PRAISE FOR
THE SAVVY GUIDE FOR GENERATIVE AI BEGINNERS

"In a time when generative AI is surrounded by hype and anxiety, Jamie DeAngelis offers clarity and a refreshingly optimistic mindset shift through a grounded, human-centered guide. This book goes beyond tips and tricks—it's a blueprint for marketers, strategists, and leaders looking to apply generative AI to deep, high-leverage work. As someone who has led enterprise launches, analyst engagements, and AI product positioning, I found myself nodding on every page—and came away with valuable new perspectives. Even the technical explanations are crisp and useful, but never overwhelming. Complex ideas like transformers, hallucinations, and RAG pipelines are made approachable without losing nuance. Smart, useful, and fun. I'm all in!"

HARINI SRIDHARAN | AI PRODUCT
MARKETING LEADER

"As someone well-versed in AI, I was initially skeptical about The Savvy Guide for Generative AI Beginners. I was wrong. I learned a great deal, especially about ways to integrate AI into organizations and to consider the ethical implications of AI in practical terms. The book successfully strikes a delicate balance —helping AI beginners gain a solid understanding of what AI is all about and apply it to achieve greater success, while also providing substance for those already in the "AI trenches." A worthy read."

BLAKE PARK | CHIEF STRATEGY OFFICER

"I am deeply grateful to Jamie for her extraordinary ability to distill complexity into clarity, particularly while we co-led transformation initiatives for global companies. Her empathy for the people behind the process, paired with a sharp intellect and mastery of language, makes her a rare voice in the evolving conversation around AI. She reminds us that technology, at its best, is a reflection of our shared humanity."

DANIELLE STRAIT | VICE PRESIDENT,
TECHNOLOGY

"As someone who's been navigating the AI transformation, I know how overwhelming it can feel to figure out where to start. This book delivers exactly what every business needs right now —practical frameworks that actually work, not just theory. It's the roadmap that every business leader needs when implementing AI across their teams."

LINDSAY BOYAJIAN HAGAN | VICE PRESIDENT,
MARKETING

As a solopreneur, I don't have a big team (or endless hours) to figure out how to make AI work for me. That's why this book is an absolute game-changer.

The Savvy Guide for Generative AI Beginners takes a topic that often feels confusing and breaks it down in a way that actually makes sense. Jamie turns something intimidating into something totally doable. It's like AI with training wheels—and you're riding by yourself in no time.

The chapter on writing better prompts alone completely changed how I use ChatGPT. I'm finally asking smarter questions and getting more effective answers faster. AI no longer feels overwhelming. It feels empowering.

And the bonuses? Next level. The *Smart Stack for Small Teams and Entrepreneurs* introduced me to tools I didn't even know existed—and better yet, explained exactly what each one is best for. Total time-saver. And the *Dear Custom GPT* guide? Pure gold. It gave me the exact steps to confidently build GPTs tailored to my needs.

Whether you run a business or just want smarter help at home, this is your starting line. Jamie, thank you for creating a guide that's not only smart, but actually usable. You nailed it!

SALLY SORICELLI | ENTREPRENEUR, EDUCATOR, INTERIOR DESIGNER

"This smart, straight-talking guide to generative AI cuts through the buzzword-heavy hype and actually makes sense. Jamie's point of view not only gave me the confidence to "talk the talk" with clients like I'd been doing it for years—but finally ditch the panic that AI is going to eat my lunch. If you're still losing sleep over AI killing your agency's pipeline, this book is a practical approach to making AI your strongest collaborator and not your biggest competition."

BETH HANIGAN | VICE PRESIDENT, CLIENT SERVICES

"Jamie's book offers a refreshing, grounded perspective. She thoughtfully unpacks the complexities of GenAI, cutting through the noise with actionable tips and invaluable insights. You'll learn how to collaborate with AI as a thought partner and idea engine—without ever losing your creative vision. Whether you're just getting started, leveling up your prompt game, or looking to supercharge your business with GenAI, this is your playbook."

GREG HICKS | TECHNICAL PROGRAM MANAGER

"The Savvy Guide for Generative AI Beginners is an ideal starting point for anyone who's curious (but maybe a bit overwhelmed) by the rise of generative AI. Jamie DeAngelis explains how the technology works and where it fits into everyday work, all in clear, relatable language. As she puts it, "To make this transition, you'll need to learn to talk to machines"—and this book gives you the confidence to do exactly that. Thoughtful, practical, and encouraging, it's your guide to exploring, experimenting, and leading in this rapidly evolving digital world."

ROBERTO LINO | CHIEF EXECUTIVE OFFICER

"If you're a marketer, strategist, team lead, or just AI-curious and tired of the hype, this book is for you. Jamie's voice is smart, funny, and refreshingly real—like getting advice from a sharp friend who's already done the hard parts. It's the perfect starting point if you want to use generative AI without losing your judgment (or your job)."

JUSTIN STAYROOK | CHIEF GROWTH OFFICER AND HEAD OF STRATEGY

"Working alongside Jamie over the years has been nothing short of inspiring. She has a rare ability to take emerging technologies like generative AI and translate them into something deeply human, practical, and creatively exciting.

Like many in the creative industry, I initially approached AI with hesitation. I wasn't sure how it fit into a process built on intuition, experience, and original thinking. But watching how Jamie applied AI in real-world strategy work helped shift my perspective. She didn't treat AI as a replacement for expertise. She showed me how it could enhance it. Her approach made it clear that my years of creative experience weren't obsolete. They were my biggest asset in guiding AI tools toward better, faster, and more thoughtful outcomes.

This book is a perfect reflection of that mindset. Jamie makes AI feel less like a black box and more like a tool you can actually use with purpose. It's approachable, honest, and full of practical insight. Whether you are just getting started or looking to scale AI across a team, her guidance meets you where you are and gives you the confidence to go further.

I'm grateful to have worked with Jamie and even more grateful for the clarity she continues to bring to such a fast-moving space."

ELISA ANGUIANO | CREATIVE DIRECTOR

"This book should be required reading for anyone navigating the impact of AI on their work. Jamie doesn't just explain generative AI—she cuts through the hype with clarity, strategy, and real-world insight to help you think faster, work smarter, and stay relevant in a changing world."

JOHN SCHNEIDER | CHIEF MARKETING OFFICER

THE SAVVY GUIDE FOR GENERATIVE AI BEGINNERS

CRAFT SMARTER PROMPTS, MANAGE RISKS, AND DRIVE AUTHENTIC, INNOVATIVE RESULTS (BEFORE AI DOES IT FOR YOU)

JAMIE DEANGELIS, PH.D.

DOUBLE PEAK
PUBLISHING

ISBN 979-8-9991290-0-0 (Paperback Edition)

ISBN 979-8-9991290-1-7 (eBook Edition – Kindle)

ISBN 979-8-9991290-2-4 (eBook Edition – EPUB)

For everyone who's ever been equal parts awed and alarmed by generative AI —this book is for you. May your prompts be sharp, your outputs useful, and your skepticism always just the right amount of spicy.

———

And for my family: Thank you for pretending to listen when I explained (again) that when AI "hallucinates," it's not daydreaming—it's just confidently making things up, like a kid telling you they definitely didn't eat the last cookie. You deserve medals. Or at least unlimited screen time.

CONTENTS

PART ONE
UNDERSTANDING GENERATIVE AI: WHAT IT IS, WHAT IT ISN'T, AND WHY IT KEEPS SAYING WEIRD THINGS ABOUT PASTA

PART TWO
LEAD THE AI—DON'T LET IT LEAD YOU

PART THREE
SCALING WHAT WORKS, WHETHER YOU'RE BOSSING THE BOARDROOM OR WEARING ALL THE HATS

PART FOUR
GETTING REALLY, REALLY GOOD AT IT

FOREWORD

A few years ago, if someone had told me that artificial intelligence would fundamentally reshape how my marketing team works—how we ideate, strategize, and even write—I would've nodded politely, then gone back to reviewing this quarter's campaign metrics. Not because I doubted AI's potential, but because it felt more like a concept than an untapped capability. Distant. Like something just over the horizon.

Not anymore.

Today, generative AI is *here*. It's not science fiction—it's a strategic imperative. And in my role as CMO at Betterworks, a company helping organizations drive performance through alignment, engagement, and continuous feedback, I've seen firsthand how AI is changing the way we operate, communicate, and deliver value.

But let me be clear: This shift isn't just about tools. It's about mindset.

That's what makes this book so essential.

Jamie DeAngelis has written the kind of guide I wish I had when I first started diving into generative AI. It's practical, grounded, and refreshingly honest about both the promise and the limitations of the technology. It doesn't hype AI as a magic solution, nor does it downplay its potential. Instead, it gives leaders and teams the context—and confidence—they need to make generative AI work *for* them.

And it couldn't come at a more critical time.

At Betterworks, marketing is a lean, fast-moving team. We don't have the luxury of massive innovation budgets or specialized AI teams. What we *do* have is curiosity, drive, and a strong belief in staying ahead of the curve—we even have fun with it. Over the past year, we've rolled up our sleeves to explore how generative AI can supercharge campaign development, sharpen our product messaging, and scale our storytelling—without sacrificing original thought or the voice of the customer. We're still learning—as any modern marketing team should be—but we're miles ahead of where we started, and a powerful resource like this book gives others the opportunity to accelerate their strategy and impact with generative AI.

This book breaks down the complexity of generative AI into something accessible, useful, and, most importantly, actionable. Jamie doesn't just teach you how to prompt an AI model—she teaches you how to think differently about your work, your skills, and your role in a rapidly evolving digital world.

If you're a leader wondering how to upskill your team without overwhelming them, read this book. If you're a leader trying to figure out where AI strategically fits into your business, start here. And if you're a practitioner who just wants to work smarter, faster, and with a little less friction, this book will show you how to do exactly that—without losing the human touch that makes your work matter, in the first place.

We're all standing at the beginning of a new chapter in how business gets done. The teams that thrive won't be the ones with the biggest budgets—but the ones bold enough to *learn, experiment, and adapt.*

If you're holding this book, that probably means you are.

You're in good hands.

JOHN SCHNEIDER
Chief Marketing Officer, Betterworks

YOUR SMART BONUSES

As a thank-you for reading *The Savvy Guide for Generative AI Beginners*, I've created three companion resources to help you turn what you've learned into action—with more clarity, less chaos, and way fewer browser tabs.

You can download all three at:
https://www.doublepeakpublishing.com/savvy-guide-ai-beginners-3-smart-bonuses

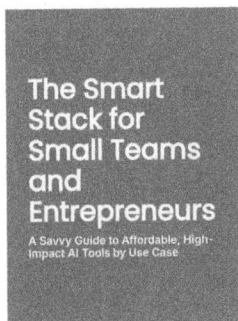

The Smart Stack for Small Teams and Entrepreneurs

A Savvy Guide to Affordable, High-impact AI Tools by Use Case

Feeling overwhelmed by the sea of AI tools out there? This curated guide helps small teams and entrepreneurs find beginner-friendly tools that actually work. It's organized by real-life use cases (like content, social, project management, and more) and includes "Best For" notes to help you choose wisely and move faster.

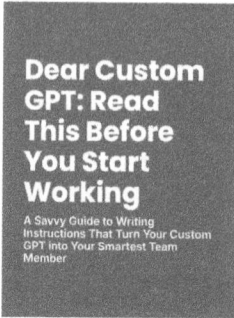

Dear Custom GPT: Read This Before You Start Working

A Savvy Guide to Writing Instructions That Turn Your Custom GPT into Your Smartest Team Member

If you're training your own custom GPT (or thinking about it), this guide will help you write better instructions, structure your knowledge, and build smarter, more reliable AI teammates. Use it to avoid common pitfalls and get real results—without needing to speak "engineer."

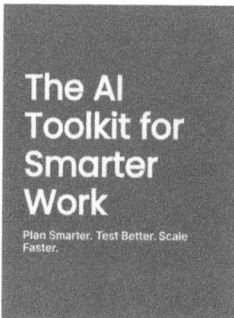

The AI Toolkit for Smarter Work

Plan Smarter. Test Better. Scale Faster.

This bonus worksheet helps you assess tools, plan and build custom GPTs, and document what's working so you can scale it. Includes plug-and-play planners, testers, and trackers—so you're not rebuilding from scratch every time you start a new AI project.

Grab your copies and start building your smarter AI stack today.
https://www.doublepeakpublishing.com/savvy-guide-ai-beginners-3-smart-bonuses

INTRODUCTION

When generative AI first hit the scene, most of us had a moment. You know the one. The *gulp*. The "Uh-oh, is this thing coming for my job?" moment.

Take Sarah, for example. She was a seasoned marketing director, the kind who could transform a spreadsheet of data into a story that actually made people *care*. Her team relied on her knack for turning dry insights into compelling narratives, guiding them through the ever-changing world of digital content.

Then, along came AI. Suddenly, the internet was filled with articles generated by algorithms, and Sarah felt a shiver of professional dread. Was a machine really going to out-write her? And not just her—what about her team? The junior writers she'd mentored, the creatives who'd honed their craft through years of practice—what did AI mean for all of them?

For a while, she did what many of us do when faced with an intimidating new technology: nothing. She ignored it. Side-eyed it. Maybe even hoped it was a fad, like neon leg warmers or diet grapefruit. But the buzz only got louder, and eventually, curiosity (and a little pressure from her boss) nudged her into action.

So, she dove in. And it wasn't exactly love at first draft. Sure, the AI could generate ideas at lightning speed, but sometimes those ideas felt more like the salad bar at a discount buffet—plenty of quantity, not so much quality. It could spit out paragraphs of text, but they often needed more finesse, more context, more *human*.

But as Sarah played around with prompts, adjusted her approach, and figured out where the tool excelled (and where it fell flat), something clicked. She stopped seeing AI as an imposter and started seeing it as a collaborator. It wasn't about letting the machine do her job—it was about using it to supercharge her creativity, speed up her process, and even push her thinking in new directions.

And here's the twist: As she got more comfortable, her initial fears started to fade. The technology wasn't flawless—far from it. But instead of settling for "good enough," Sarah's curiosity took over. She wanted to know *why* the AI worked the way it did, why it sometimes missed the mark, and how understanding its mechanisms and limitations could help her unlock its full potential. She became a bit of a detective, diving into the *why* behind the technology, convinced that this deeper knowledge was the key to getting the best out of her new AI teammate.

Instead of a threat, AI became an opportunity. Sarah remained the expert, but now she had a powerful, if sometimes awkward, new team member. She learned to guide the AI, to ask better questions, and to use its capabilities to enhance her work, not replace it. And in the end, it reshaped not just how she worked but also how she thought about her role in a world where technology and creativity increasingly intersect.

AI FREAKED ME OUT, TOO (UNTIL IT DIDN'T)

Okay, confession time: Sarah is actually me. I know, I know—plot twist! But the truth is, everything I just shared wasn't a story from afar; it was my story. I had that same *gulp* moment, the same anxiety over whether AI might swoop in and do my job better, faster, and with fewer coffee breaks.

When I first started using AI, it felt a lot like playing one of my son's video games on hard mode—with the instructions in another language. I leaned on every tactic and template I could find, but the results were ... let's just say, *inconsistent*. There were moments of brilliance, sure, but also more than a few, "Wait, what is this even talking about?" moments.

But I'm not one to back away from a challenge. I decided if I was going to make this work, I needed to do more than just dabble. I adopted an intentional learning mindset. I sat down with AI engineers, asked a lot of questions (some of them pretty basic, I'll admit), took technical courses, and became a bit of a detective—digging into the *why* behind the technology. I wanted to understand not just how to use AI but how it really worked. And slowly but surely, those pieces started to click into place.

In case we haven't met yet, I'm Jamie DeAngelis. I'm the Head of Brand Strategy and Content and the architect and leader of the Generative AI Center of Excellence at a leading digital agency. I've spent my career at the intersection of technology, creativity, and innovation—building strategies that help teams and businesses adapt and succeed in evolving markets and digital landscapes. My background spans diverse industries and countless projects, and for over a decade, I also taught at UC Berkeley, earning two teaching effectiveness awards along the way. I love making complex ideas accessible and actionable, and mentoring others to adapt and excel in this fast-paced world.

Embracing generative AI was a turning point not just for my work but for how I saw my role. AI didn't take my job, but it definitely reshaped it. I found myself collaborating with AI engineering teams, contributing to training systems, designing prompts, and preparing unstructured data for AI applications. The shift was profound. What started as a survival tactic became a strategic advantage, pushing me to apply my expertise in brand and content strategy in entirely new and impactful ways.

Today, AI is like my work sidekick. It's not perfect (and, let's be real, neither am I), but together we've managed to turn a lot of those initial frustrations into a wellspring of creativity and efficiency. And that's exactly what this book is all about—helping you move from that *gulp* moment to a place of genuine confidence and competence with AI.

IS THIS BOOK FOR YOU? (PROBABLY.)

So, who exactly is this book for? Well, if you've ever stared at your computer, wondering if an AI might do your job faster—or if you've secretly hoped that wasn't the case—this book is for you. It's for professionals, entrepreneurs, and leaders trying to make sense of the generative AI whirlwind. Whether you're looking to integrate AI into your workflow, tackle those "Why does this AI keep giving me nonsense?" moments, or upskill your team, this guide has you covered.

At the heart of this journey is what I like to call the *AI Mindset Shift*. It's all about rethinking how you approach work, seeing AI not as a job-stealing robot but as your smartest (and perhaps most literal) coworker. Imagine working alongside AI much like you would with a team of sharp colleagues. Generative AI can pitch ideas, generate drafts, or analyze data—while you bring the judgment, creativity, and context that only humans can provide. It's not here to write, design, or think for you—unless you hand over the keys (which I wouldn't advise). You get to stay in the driver's seat. The magic happens when *you* choose to write, design, and think *with* AI—on your terms, with your voice, and your vision leading the way.

If that sounds a bit futuristic, well, so did assembly lines and personal computers in their day. When the first assembly lines rolled out, people worried about the loss of craftsmanship and jobs—and, yes, some jobs did go away. But manufacturing was revolutionized, productivity soared, and entirely new roles emerged. The same happened with personal computers. Sure, some traditional office tasks were automated, but the shift also gave rise to whole new fields like IT and software development. Generative AI is following a similar path. It's true that AI will change the nature of work, and that can feel a little unsettling. But history shows us that those who adapt—who learn to incorporate new technologies into their roles and evolve along with them—are the ones who thrive. Generative AI, when applied strategically and ethically, has the potential to transform challenges into opportunities and open doors to innovations we haven't yet imagined.

But here's the catch: To make this transition, you'll need to learn to talk to machines. This is a skill distinct from human interaction but no less empowering. Mastering this new language—and understanding both the perks and the pitfalls of generative AI—will prepare you to use it responsibly and effectively. It's about solving real problems, driving meaningful results, and building AI literacy. Just like digital literacy became essential in the age of the internet, AI literacy is now a must-have skill in today's world. And if you're ready to embrace this shift, you'll find yourself on the leading edge of innovation and impact.

HERE'S WHAT YOU'LL ACTUALLY LEARN

If you're looking for quick hacks or a 5-day mastery plan, this isn't that book. (And, spoiler alert: Anyone promising that is probably selling something sketchy.) Instead, this book is all about building a solid foundation—a deep, lasting understanding of generative AI that goes beyond surface-level tricks.

This book embraces a teach-don't-tell philosophy. We're not just covering the *how* of AI but digging into the *why*. Why does it work the way it does? Why does it sometimes miss the mark? Why is crafting the right prompt the difference between brilliance and, well, a total head-scratcher? And why do you even need to know that? Because knowing the *why* is what transforms generative AI from a novelty into a powerful, results-driven tool that can elevate your work and your thinking.

The chapters are designed to build on each other, layer by layer—from foundational knowledge to strategic application to creative mastery. Here's what you'll learn along the way:

- **The basics of generative AI**: Not just how it works, but why it matters to your work.
- **Core principles to align AI with your goals**: Because the best outputs start with the right inputs.
- **How to use AI responsibly**: Including ethics, risks, and frameworks for smart, human-centered decisions.

- **Ways to scale AI in your business or team**: Whether you're working solo or leading a full transformation.
- **How to craft smarter prompts**: Unlocking more impactful, relevant, and creative results.
- **Collaborating with AI like a pro**: Making it your sidekick, not your replacement.
- **Flexible frameworks and real-world scenarios**: So you can adapt what you learn across any tool, role, or industry.

This isn't just about learning tactics—it's about moving from dabbling to doing it right. I've distilled my experience (and a lot of trial and error) into clear, actionable guidance. By the end, you'll feel confident and capable, ready to navigate this transformative technology with the skill and savvy of a true pro.

READY? LET'S DO THIS.

Generative AI isn't a passing trend—it's here to stay. And those who lean in early, who get comfortable with the uncomfortable, will be the ones leading the charge. This book is your guide to working smarter, thinking bigger, and staying ahead of the curve. Whether you're here to level up your workflow or just keep from feeling like you're stuck in the AI slow lane, the journey starts here. Let's dive in and get to work.

PART ONE

UNDERSTANDING GENERATIVE AI: WHAT IT IS, WHAT IT ISN'T, AND WHY IT KEEPS SAYING WEIRD THINGS ABOUT PASTA

Before you can use generative AI well, you need to actually understand what the heck it is—and what it isn't. This part unpacks the basics without the jargon and busts the myths that make smart people hesitate.

ONE

WAIT, WHAT IS GENERATIVE AI, EXACTLY?

G enerative AI. It's the tech everyone's talking about—but let's be honest: For many, it still feels like a bit of a mystery. Sure, you've heard it can write articles, design logos, brainstorm names, and maybe even whip up a decent recipe for chocolate chip cookies. But what exactly *is* generative AI? How does it actually work? And, most importantly, how do *you* make it work for you?

Think of this chapter as your backstage pass. It won't just show you the big stage tricks—it'll reveal what's happening behind the curtain, so you can use this technology with more confidence, creativity, and intention. Because here's the thing: Generative AI isn't one thing or another until *we* decide what to do with it. It doesn't act on its own. It reflects how we prompt it, guide it, train it, and govern it. Whether you're an entrepreneur, a creative pro, or a decision-maker navigating change, understanding how this technology works puts you in the driver's seat. And with that understanding, you're better equipped to shape its role—avoiding common stumbles, unlocking fresh possibilities, and contributing to a smarter, more thoughtful use of AI in your corner of the world.

I learned this the hard way. When I first started working with generative AI, I felt like I was missing some secret ingredient. I copied prompts from tutorials. I watched the how-to webinars. But half the time, the results fell flat—and I had no idea how to fix them. The issue wasn't the tool; it was that I didn't understand *why* it behaved the way it did. And without that knowledge, I couldn't troubleshoot or adapt it to what I actually needed.

Eventually, I got curious and dug deeper. I talked to AI engineers. I took technical courses. I learned just enough to understand how the thing thinks. That one shift—from surface-level tactics to foundational fluency—made all the difference. Suddenly I wasn't guessing anymore. I was guiding. My prompts worked better, my ideas and applications got sharper, and my results were actually aligned with what I needed.

This isn't just a personal story. Across industries, I've watched teams lock down AI tools out of fear or skip over them because no one understands what's under the hood. That's a missed opportunity—and it's usually avoidable. You don't need to be an engineer or a data scientist to use generative AI well. But a little understanding? That goes a long way.

By the end of this chapter, you won't just know *what* generative AI is—you'll understand *how* it works and *why* that matters. This isn't about learning to code or memorizing jargon. It's about building just enough technical fluency to use AI well—and use it wisely. Because when you know what's happening under the hood, you're not just a passenger along for the ride. You're a collaborator, a guide, and maybe even a steward of how this technology shows up in your life, your work, and your industry.

1.1 GENERATIVE AI 101 (BUT MAKE IT ACTUALLY USEFUL)

Generative AI is a game-changer in the world of artificial intelligence. Unlike earlier AI tools that were all about following instructions, generative AI brings something new to the table—creativity and innovation. To understand just how significant this shift is, let's take a quick walk through AI's evolution.

Early AI systems were rule-based, like a glorified calculator. You'd input a command, and they'd spit out a response based on a set of programmed rules. They were reliable but not exactly imaginative. Then came machine learning, which took things up a notch. These systems could learn from data, getting better over time without needing to be reprogrammed for every new task. Deep learning pushed even further, using neural networks to analyze vast amounts of data and spot complex patterns that humans might miss.

And then, generative AI stepped onto the scene. This isn't just a tool that interprets the world—it contributes to it. Whether it's writing text, generating images, composing music, or more, generative AI doesn't just react to input; it creates something new. That's a huge leap forward, shifting AI's role from a reactive assistant to a proactive partner in creativity and innovation.

To make the distinction clear, think of traditional AI as a really sharp assistant. It can analyze your data, follow instructions, and help you make decisions based on logic and learned patterns. Think of systems like customer service chatbots that follow pre-programmed scripts, or recommendation engines that serve up products based on your past behavior. They're helpful, but they're not exactly brimming with new ideas. Generative AI, on the other hand, is more like a creative collaborator. It doesn't just answer questions—it imagines possibilities. Tools like ChatGPT and DALL·E are prime examples, generating human-like text and entirely original images that can inspire fresh directions, unexpected angles, and new ways of thinking.

Generative AI shines brightest in areas that thrive on creativity and adaptability. It can transform marketing by generating campaign ideas, enhance customer experiences with highly personalized interactions, and even become your brainstorming buddy when you need fresh perspectives. But it's not a magic wand. Tasks that require precision and reliability—like robotic automation or air traffic control—are still better suited for traditional AI or non-AI systems. And let's be honest: Generative AI can occasionally miss the mark. It's not your go-to for exact outputs, such as legal document analysis or complex calculations where accuracy is critical.

That's where pairing generative AI with predictive machine learning models can lead to the best of both worlds. Imagine a customer service setup where generative AI crafts personalized responses while predictive models analyze customer sentiment and behavior based on historical data and trends—or where generative AI itself adapts its tone and content based on real-time sentiment cues. The result? A blend of creativity and precision that can elevate user experiences and help businesses not just meet but exceed expectations. Plus, generative AI's natural language abilities make complex tech more approachable, opening doors for more people to engage with advanced systems across industries.

WHY THIS MATTERS

Understanding where generative AI fits within the broader AI ecosystem is a game-changer for anyone who wants to use it well. Without that clarity, it's easy to get swept up in the hype—or write it off entirely. Some people hear *generative AI* and assume it's some kind of *general* AI, capable of doing everything. That misconception can lead to disappointment when the technology doesn't nail accuracy or specificity. Others assume it's just a fancy autocomplete, missing out on its ability to generate creative, contextually rich outputs. Neither view is quite right, and both can lead to frustration or missed opportunities.

When you grasp the difference between traditional AI and generative AI, you start seeing each tool for what it actually is—and isn't. You stop expecting generative AI to deliver perfect facts or perform surgical-level accuracy. Instead, you start tapping into what it *is* great at: generating creative outputs, drafting from scratch, brainstorming new directions, and helping you explore ideas quickly. That shift in mindset is what unlocks real results.

Here's what that looks like in practice: You're leading a product launch. Instead of asking generative AI to write your press release word-for-word (and expecting it to get every fact right), you ask it to generate five distinct angles for the announcement. Or you use it to brainstorm social captions that sound less stiff and more human. You bring the strategy and direction. The AI brings the momentum.

Understanding these distinctions also gives you a better read on where AI belongs in your workflow—and where it doesn't. You'll avoid the common traps (like using it for highly sensitive legal text), and you'll be quicker to spot the real opportunities (like using it to explore a brand voice or build quick first drafts).

Bottom line? When you know what kind of AI you're working with, you make smarter choices. You can guide it with intention. And that's what turns it from a novelty into a real, practical tool in your hands.

1.2 WHAT'S ACTUALLY GOING ON UNDER THE HOOD?

To really make generative AI work for you, it helps to understand what's going on under the hood. At its core, generative AI relies on three main components: training data, models, and outputs. Think of it like baking a cake—training data is your ingredients, models are the recipe, and outputs are the final product.

Training data is the fuel for AI. It's the massive collection of text, images, audio, and other data that the AI system analyzes to recognize patterns and make predictions. The quality and diversity of this data matter—a lot. If the data is biased or too narrow, the AI's outputs might come out half-baked (or worse, totally off the mark).

Models act as the blueprints. They're the algorithms and mathematical structures that transform raw data into something meaningful. Different models yield different results. General models, like those behind popular chatbots, are versatile and can handle a wide range of topics. But this broad approach can sometimes lead to shallow responses in specialized areas. Domain-specific models, on the other hand, dive deeper into particular subjects, offering more precision and expertise.

When it comes to size, models vary too. Large models can process massive datasets and generate complex, nuanced outputs—but they also demand significant computing power. Smaller models are more efficient and accessible, but they might not have the same depth or sophistication.

For businesses looking to get the best of both worlds, techniques like Retrieval-Augmented Generation (RAG) can bridge the gap. RAG allows developers to combine generative AI with external databases or proprietary data, making the AI smarter and more aligned with specific needs. Imagine training an AI with your company's knowledge base so its responses consistently reflect your brand's voice and expertise.

The magic happens when you integrate generative AI with other internal systems or data platforms. This approach transforms AI into a dynamic, interactive tool rather than just a creative generator. Consider a healthcare organization that combines generative AI with its patient care system. Instead of static software or rigid reports, a doctor could ask, "What are the most common symptoms among patients with similar medical histories to this one?" The AI, tapping into both the generative model and the healthcare data, could provide actionable insights, helping healthcare professionals make faster, more informed decisions.

Or take a manufacturing company that pairs generative AI with its operational analytics platform. Instead of wading through static dashboards, employees could ask open-ended questions like, "What trends in equipment downtime have emerged over the past quarter?" The AI could analyze the data, summarize key insights, and even suggest optimizations—making it easier to turn raw data into real action.

WHY THIS MATTERS

Knowing how training data, models, and outputs work together doesn't just make you sound smarter in meetings—it helps you actually get better results from generative AI. Without that understanding, it's easy to misinterpret what the AI gives you, or worse, trust outputs that are biased, off-base, or just plain wrong. But when you understand how it thinks—what it's drawing from, how it's structured, and where its limits are—you can guide it more effectively and use it more responsibly.

For example, if you understand that a general-purpose model has limits, you won't expect it to answer specialized questions with perfect accuracy. You'll know when to bring in domain-specific tools or add guardrails like RAG to make it smarter. You'll start to see prompts not as magic spells, but as levers you can pull to tune the system toward your goals.

This foundation also opens up customization. You might not be building models from scratch, but maybe you're experimenting with a custom GPT. If you know how training data affects voice and tone, you'll feed it examples that reflect your brand. If you understand model architecture at a high level, you'll be better equipped to troubleshoot odd behavior—or know when it's time to escalate to a tech partner.

The bottom line? This is the difference between using AI *at* work versus putting AI *to work* for you. And when you know how it works, you're better positioned to shape how it performs, scale it smartly, and keep it aligned with your values.

1.3 NEURAL NETWORKS, TRANSFORMERS, AND OTHER SURPRISINGLY COOL STUFF

Generative AI might seem like magic, but at its core, it's powered by some very real (and really cool) technologies—namely, neural networks and transformers. These are the brains behind the operation, giving AI its ability to learn, generate, and adapt.

Neural networks are where it all started. They're modeled after the human brain, using layers of interconnected nodes (think of them as digital neurons) to process information and recognize patterns. This is how AI learns from data—whether it's identifying objects in images or predicting the next word in a sentence. It's the backbone of AI's ability to turn raw data into meaningful content.

But then came transformers, and they were a total game-changer. Traditional models could only process data in a linear, step-by-step way, but transformers broke that mold. They can analyze entire sequences of data all at once, making them incredibly efficient for tasks like text generation and language translation.

The real power behind transformers is something called the attention mechanism. When you read a sentence and come across the word "model," your brain naturally uses context to decide whether it means a fashion model or an AI system. Attention lets the AI do the same—it helps the model focus on the most relevant parts of the input to understand what's going on. Instead of treating each word in isolation, the model weighs the importance of all the surrounding words. That's what gives transformer-based tools like ChatGPT their uncanny ability to generate text that's coherent, relevant, and sounds like it was written by a real person.

This context-aware design is what allows today's generative AI to move beyond simple word prediction and into the realm of meaningful communication. It's not just filling in the blanks—it's considering the bigger picture. And that's a big part of why these tools feel less like machines and more like collaborators.

WHY THIS MATTERS

When you understand how transformers work—especially the way they use context and attention—you become way more effective at steering generative AI. This isn't about memorizing technical specs. It's about unlocking better results with fewer frustrations.

Let's say you're prompting a model to summarize a long email thread for your team. If you understand that transformers evaluate the *whole sequence* of words, not just one at a time, you can structure your input more intentionally. You might front-load key points, repeat important names, or separate topics clearly to help the AI follow your logic. That's prompt engineering in action—and it works better when you know how the machine is reading the room.

The attention mechanism is especially important. It's what helps the AI focus on the right words at the right time, and what makes responses sound coherent instead of random. If you know how that works, you're better equipped to troubleshoot when the model loses the plot—and better able to lead it back.

Even if you never touch a neural network or tweak a parameter, understanding how these systems prioritize and process language makes you a sharper user. It gives you more control over the tone, accuracy, and usefulness of your outputs. In short: It helps you stop guessing and start collaborating with AI in a way that actually gets you what you need. And don't worry—we'll dive deeper into how to craft great prompts in a later chapter. For now, just know that understanding how transformers work is the first step toward using them with confidence and skill.

1.4 GENERATIVE AI DOESN'T *KNOW*—IT PREDICTS

Generative AI doesn't *know* facts the way humans do. Instead, it's more like a super-smart pattern detective. It doesn't remember information or hold knowledge—it just analyzes patterns in its training data and uses those patterns to predict what comes next. If you've ever had your phone suggest the next word in a text message, you've seen a basic version of this at work. Generative AI is that concept on steroids —able to generate entire stories, images, and ideas based on patterns it has learned.

Here's how it works: Generative AI breaks inputs into tiny pieces called tokens. These tokens could be words, parts of words, punctuation marks, or even elements of images. The AI then encodes these tokens as vectors in a multidimensional space—think of it as plotting them on a super-complex 3D map. Similar concepts are grouped together, so colors like "red," "blue," and "green" might sit close to each other because they often share similar contexts as colors.

What makes generative AI particularly unique is its ability to introduce a bit of randomness into its predictions. Unlike traditional systems that always go with the most likely answer, generative AI occasionally takes a less-traveled path, leading to creative and sometimes surprising results. For example, if you type "The cat climbed up the…" into a generative AI model, it might choose "tree" as the most likely next word. But it could also surprise you with "stairs," "roof," or even "mountain," adding a creative twist that a standard predictive system would never attempt.

This randomness is controlled by a setting called "temperature." A low temperature setting keeps things predictable—great for when you need accuracy and consistency, like in technical writing. A higher temperature makes the AI more adventurous, which can be perfect for brainstorming or creative projects where you want fresh, unexpected ideas.

Imagine you're writing a story and need a plot twist. With a higher temperature setting, generative AI might suggest something completely out of the box—like your character finding a hidden door in a mundane office setting. This feature mirrors the way humans think creatively, exploring the less obvious paths that sometimes lead to groundbreaking ideas.

However, this same randomness can also lead to less precise outputs, which isn't ideal for tasks that require strict accuracy—like financial analysis or legal documentation. When precision matters, developers often use techniques like fine-tuning (teaching the AI specific information to keep it focused) or retrieval-based methods (connecting the AI to external data) to keep it on track.

Why This Matters

When you understand that generative AI isn't retrieving facts but predicting patterns, everything clicks into place. Suddenly, those quirky or off-base answers make more sense. You're no longer expecting an encyclopedia; you're working with a high-powered improviser.

This mindset shift changes how you use the technology. Instead of asking it to deliver airtight answers, you ask it to explore ideas. Instead of assuming a weird response means the *AI doesn't know,* you recognize that it's making its best guess based on patterns—and sometimes those guesses can be surprisingly creative or subtly flawed.

That awareness also helps you understand why the AI sometimes plays it safe—and other times surprises you with a wild idea. Behind the scenes, settings like "temperature" influence how predictable or creative the responses are. While you might not have direct control over those dials in everyday tools, just knowing they exist helps you make better choices about *how* you interact with the AI. Want fresh, out-of-the-box thinking? Use open-ended prompts. Need consistency? Be more specific and structured. Either way, you're guiding the tone—even if you're not adjusting the actual settings. And when you pair this understanding with tools like fine-tuning or retrieval methods, you can balance creativity with control.

Even if you're not the one doing the technical work, you'll be better equipped to understand the tools you're working with (and how you should apply them), ask the right questions, request the right features, and steer the tech toward outcomes that serve your goals.

Bottom line: The more you understand how generative AI *thinks*, the less you're reacting to its behavior—and the more you're shaping it to match your needs.

1.5 KNOW WHEN TO CALL IN THE AI (AND WHEN NOT TO)

Generative AI isn't a one-size-fits-all solution—and it's definitely not a magic wand for perfect answers or bulletproof accuracy. Where it really shines is in spaces that benefit from creativity, flexibility, and pattern recognition. Used well, it can be a powerful thinking partner. Used carelessly, it can create more confusion than clarity.

Think of generative AI as a creative collaborator. It's great at brainstorming ideas, drafting unique content, and uncovering patterns—especially when you give it direction. Say you're launching a new marketing campaign. You might ask AI for tagline ideas, visual concepts, or social copy. It's like having a brainstorming partner who never runs out of steam. But remember: While the AI can explore creative directions, it's still up to *you* to define the strategy and make sure everything aligns with your goals, audience, and brand.

To make the most of it, ask yourself:

- **What do I want to achieve?** Be clear on your goal to know if generative AI is the right fit.
- **Does this task need creativity or consistency?** If you need originality, generative AI is your tool. If you need precision, consider other options.
- **How will I guide it?** Generative AI depends on your guidance to deliver relevant and useful results. The more specific and structured your prompt, the more useful the output.

For example, generative AI is a great partner when you're ideating or writing a first draft. But when accuracy is critical—say, with financial disclosures or compliance documents—it's not the right tool to fly solo. Use your judgment. Match the tool to the task.

At its best, generative AI helps you work faster, think more expansively, and iterate with ease. Whether it replaces or elevates your expertise isn't up to the technology—it's up to how you choose to use it. With intention, it becomes a partner. Without it, a shortcut that can easily go sideways.

In the next chapter, we'll tackle some of the biggest myths and misconceptions about generative AI—so you can separate fact from fiction, sidestep the hype (and the fear), and move forward with a clearer, more confident sense of what this technology can actually do for you.

TWO

MYTHS, MISUNDERSTANDINGS, AND THAT ONE WILD AI MEETING

f you've ever been in a meeting where the conversation takes an unexpected left turn, you'll know exactly how I felt that day. What was supposed to be a straightforward project wrap-up turned into a crash course on generative AI misconceptions. We'd been working on a generative AI tool designed to streamline customer interactions for a large enterprise. The project team was small and dedicated, and everything seemed to be on track. So, when we scheduled the final call, we expected a quick and easy sign-off.

Then the meeting started, and instead of a small group, more than forty stakeholders showed up—from risk and compliance to marketing and IT. Their questions came in fast and furious, and suddenly, it was clear we were not all on the same page.

Can our AI tool pull information from our competitors and present it to our clients?

Will this tool give customers personal information about our employees?

What's the hallucination rate of the large language model we're using?

These questions weren't just about curiosity—they revealed deep-seated myths and misunderstandings about what generative AI can and cannot do. It became clear that while our project team had been focused on building and implementing the solution, the broader organization had missed out on some key foundational knowledge. And that gap could lead to real problems—skepticism, fear, and, ultimately, roadblocks to progress.

Generative AI is powerful, but it's not magic. It has limitations, and understanding these boundaries is critical to using it effectively. That meeting was a wake-up call, a reminder that successful AI implementation isn't just about the technology itself—it's also about education, alignment, and setting realistic expectations with every stakeholder involved.

In this chapter, we're going to dive into some of the most common myths about generative AI. We'll sort fact from fiction, clarify what AI can and can't do, and help you build a clearer, more practical understanding of how to use this technology to its full potential—without the confusion, fear, or unrealistic expectations.

2.1 MISCONCEPTION #1: HALLUCINATIONS MEAN AI IS BROKEN

If you've spent any time with generative AI, you've likely seen it: an AI-generated response that sounds spot-on but is actually ... completely wrong. This phenomenon is called an *AI hallucination,* and it's one of the most misunderstood aspects of generative AI. The myth? That these hallucinations are just bugs that will be fixed as the technology improves. But here's the truth: AI hallucination isn't a glitch—it's a feature of how generative AI works.

Let's break it down. Generative AI is built on probabilities. When it responds to a prompt, it's not retrieving facts from a database. It's predicting the next word (or token) in a sentence based on the patterns it learned during training. Sometimes that means you get a beautifully coherent, relevant, and even creative answer. Other times, it takes a creative detour into wrong-ville, confidently handing you a nugget of nonsense wrapped in a bow. This is especially likely if the AI encounters a gap in its training data or if the input prompt is vague or open-ended.

This unpredictability isn't a flaw to be squashed out of existence. Generative AI thrives on a bit of randomness—it's what allows the technology to surprise us with new ideas, unusual phrasing, or unexpected creativity. But that same randomness is also why you sometimes get an AI response that makes you go, "Wait, what?"

WHAT THIS MEANS FOR YOU

Generative AI is not your all-knowing oracle. It's your brainstorm buddy. Your rough-draft generator. Your "help me think this through" sidekick.

Here's how to work with it, not against it:

- **Always review before you rely.** Think of AI content as a starting point, not the final word. If you're using it for anything that matters—client-facing, strategy-setting, or fact-heavy—put on your editor hat and check its work.
- **Lower the temperature when you need precision.** The "temperature" setting controls how creative or focused an AI's responses are—lower values make it more predictable and precise, while higher values increase creativity and variation. This setting is generally only available in advanced configurations or through API use, not in standard off-the-shelf ChatGPT experiences. If you're working with custom tools or enterprise systems, adjusting temperature can be a helpful lever for improving accuracy.
- **Use retrieval-augmented generation (RAG) in custom enterprise systems.** This fancy term just means you're giving your AI a specific, trusted library to pull from—like your company knowledge base or internal wiki. It's a great way to keep the AI grounded in your reality. Retrieval-augmented generation is typically implemented by engineering teams or built into enterprise-level systems, but individuals and small businesses can create custom GPTs

through platforms like OpenAI, which can replicate some of the benefits of enterprise RAG systems using curated content libraries or proprietary documents.

- **Apply smaller, specialized models (SLMs) in sensitive industries.** These domain-specific models are trained on a narrow set of info—legal, medical, finance, you name it—so they're more accurate where it counts. Again, these models are typically part of a custom AI build, not your everyday tool.

AI hallucinations aren't going away. But they don't have to derail your workflow, either. When you know how to spot them and manage them, they become less of a dealbreaker and more of a quirky trait you plan for—like autocorrect with a creative streak.

2.2 MISCONCEPTION #2: AI SECRETLY PULLS DATA FROM PLACES IT SHOULDN'T

One common concern I hear from business leaders dipping their toes into generative AI is this: "What if it pulls information from competitors? Or uses our proprietary data without permission?" It's a valid concern, and it taps into broader anxieties around data privacy and intellectual property. But the truth is, generative AI doesn't have a secret back door to your competitors' data—or to any external data, for that matter—unless it's specifically programmed to do so.

Generative AI works by analyzing patterns in its training data and generating new, original content based on those patterns. It doesn't secretly scrape or copy private data that wasn't given to it. Think of it more like a chef who's tasted thousands of dishes and uses that experience to create something new—not a cook who's sneaking into a competitor's kitchen and copying the recipe.

However, this doesn't mean there are no ethical or legal considerations. It's true that many of the original large language models were trained on publicly available data—including books, websites, and images—without explicit permission from the creators. This has sparked heated debates (and legal battles) over data usage and copyright. It's a gray area that's still being hashed out. So while generative AI doesn't autonomously steal information, responsible use *does* require thoughtful boundaries and clear governance.

<h3 style="text-align:center">WHAT THIS MEANS FOR YOU</h3>

Generative AI doesn't go rogue with your data or your competitors'. But how it behaves depends on how it's configured and used. Here's how to stay on the right side of both ethics and practicality:

- **Understand your tool's access level.** Some tools—like ChatGPT with web browsing enabled or Google Gemini—can pull information from the open web in real time. Others operate purely on pre-trained data. Either way, these tools cannot access private databases or proprietary competitor information unless they've been explicitly connected to such sources. Also, keep in mind that different AI platforms (and even different subscription tiers within the same platform) have varying policies around how your inputs are handled. Some may use your prompts and responses to further train their models unless you're on a plan that opts you out of data sharing. Always review the data usage and privacy settings in your tool—and when in doubt, avoid inputting anything sensitive.
- **Use Retrieval-Augmented Generation (RAG) for internal knowledge.** With enterprise tools, you can programmatically connect your AI to trusted data sources—like internal documents, wikis, or databases—so that its responses reflect what *you* want it to know. This doesn't happen by default; it takes deliberate setup by engineers or platform providers.
- **Don't expect it to gather proprietary competitive intelligence.** AI can synthesize insights from what it has learned, but it can't access a competitor's secure information or extract proprietary strategy docs—because AI can't (and

shouldn't) access information that even people aren't legally or ethically allowed to retrieve.

- **Establish clear guidelines for ethical use.** Just because AI *can* generate something doesn't mean it *should*. Whether you're generating copy, images, or code, build internal policies that define how AI tools should be used, reviewed, and attributed.

Used well, AI becomes a collaborative partner—creative, fast, and surprisingly helpful. Used carelessly, it can raise red flags with legal, compliance, or customers. The key is transparency, clear boundaries, and a healthy dose of digital ethics. That's how you harness the upside without drifting into the danger zone.

2.3 MISCONCEPTION #3: AI HAS A MIND OF ITS OWN

If you've ever seen a sci-fi movie, you might think AI is just a step away from running the world. It's a common myth that generative AI is fully autonomous and uncontrollable—that once you set it loose, it's off doing its own thing. But the truth is, AI is much more like a high-powered tool than a free-thinking entity. It needs guardrails, guidelines, and, yes, a human in the loop to ensure it stays on track—for now at least.

The misconception often comes from seeing tools like ChatGPT or AI agents complete complex, multi-step tasks with minimal guidance. It feels like magic. But behind the scenes, these systems follow rules, constraints, and boundaries set by the humans who built or configured them. They can't initiate action on their own. They don't form goals. They don't *want* anything. They're powerful tools—not sentient entities.

Even agentic AI systems—those designed to handle multi-step operations like summarizing reports, drafting emails, or conducting research—are guided by parameters. Engineers define their capabilities, monitor their behavior, and intervene when needed. It's a bit like setting up a GPS: The AI maps the route, but a human still sets the destination and decides whether to follow the suggested path.

WHAT THIS MEANS FOR YOU

AI isn't a runaway train. It's a really fast, really powerful train—but you're still the conductor. Here's how to keep it that way:

- **Set clear boundaries.** Define what the AI is allowed to do and what's off-limits. This can include the types of content it can generate, the data it's allowed to access, or the level of autonomy it's permitted.
- **Use human-in-the-loop design.** Especially for high-impact or customer-facing tasks, build workflows where human review and approval are required before anything gets published, shared, or implemented.
- **Monitor its behavior.** Regularly check on how your AI tools are performing. Are they staying within their guardrails? Are they delivering useful, accurate, and appropriate outputs? Think of it as routine maintenance for your AI systems.
- **Establish a governance framework.** If you're deploying AI at scale, create internal policies for how it's selected, tested, deployed, and evaluated. Include protocols for when things go sideways—because even well-behaved AI needs a plan B.

AI isn't going off the rails. But like any powerful technology, it needs oversight. When we build, use, and monitor it thoughtfully, we stay firmly in control—and unlock far more of its value along the way.

2.4 MISCONCEPTION #4: AI KNOWS WHAT IT'S TALKING ABOUT

Have you ever asked ChatGPT a tough question and gotten an answer so well-written and confident that you thought, "Wow, this thing really knows what it's talking about"? It's a common reaction. Generative AI is impressively articulate. But here's the catch: It doesn't actually *know* anything.

Generative AI doesn't have beliefs, understanding, or opinions. It doesn't reason or reflect. It doesn't draw conclusions based on real-world experience or insight. What it does is generate text by predicting the next likely word in a sequence, based on patterns it learned from massive amounts of data. That's it. It's not thinking—it's pattern-matching at scale.

But because its responses sound human and are often useful, we naturally assume there must be something deeper going on. That illusion of intelligence is part of the magic—and part of the danger. When we mistake fluency for comprehension, we risk trusting AI in situations where judgment, context, and critical thinking are essential.

What This Means for You

AI can be a powerful collaborator, but it needs a human partner to make meaning out of its outputs. Here's how to keep its strengths in perspective:

- **Always fact-check.** Even if the answer sounds right, verify it —especially if you're using AI for research, strategy, or anything sensitive. The confidence of the response doesn't equal accuracy.
- **Use it for first drafts or exploring new directions—not for making final decisions.** Let AI help you generate ideas, spot patterns, or even suggest refinements to your own work. But when it comes to choosing a direction, making a judgment call, or aligning with your goals? That's your job.
- **Lean into human context.** AI doesn't know your audience, your brand, or your business context unless you explicitly provide it—and even then, it doesn't understand it the way you do. Use your judgment to adapt and refine.
- **Watch for bias and gaps.** Because AI learns from data created by humans, it can reflect our biases or reinforce outdated assumptions. Don't assume it's neutral or complete. Bring your critical lens.

When you remember that AI is not an expert, but a clever simulator, you use it more effectively. You don't rely on it to "know" things—you use it to help you think better, faster, and more creatively. That's the sweet spot of the human-AI partnership.

2.5 MISCONCEPTION #5: AI IS ALWAYS RIGHT (BECAUSE IT SOUNDS LIKE IT)

It's ironic, really. On one end of the spectrum, people don't trust generative AI because it sometimes makes things up. On the other end, people trust it *too much* because it sounds so confident. But here's the truth: Generative AI is neither a compulsive liar nor a flawless genius. It's a probability machine.

When generative AI gives you a response, it isn't pulling a fact from a database or consulting a mental model. It's predicting what comes next based on patterns in its training data. And while that process can lead to some impressively accurate and insightful content, it can just as easily produce something outdated, biased, or flat-out wrong.

That said, it's important to clarify that we're talking here about *pure* generative AI—tools that rely solely on language models trained to generate responses based on likelihood, not verified facts.

In enterprise settings, however, it's entirely possible to build systems that combine generative AI with other types of AI or traditional software services—like search engines, databases, or logic-based automation. These systems often use something called function calling or API integration, which allows the generative AI to hand off parts of the task to another system that's purpose-built to retrieve accurate, real-time information. To the end user, it still feels like a conversation with a smart chatbot. But behind the scenes, there's a highly orchestrated process happening—where generative AI is just one player on the team.

This distinction matters. Because while off-the-shelf generative AI may not be factually reliable on its own, generative AI *can* be part of a highly accurate system when used in the right architecture. The challenge is that most users won't see what's happening behind the curtain. So it's up to AI practitioners, developers, and business leaders to ensure those systems are engineered with integrity and designed to deliver not just fluent responses, but factual ones.

This is especially tricky because generative AI doesn't hedge. It delivers information in a tone that's polished and authoritative—even when it's off-base. So if you're not double-checking, it's easy to get misled by an answer that *sounds* solid but doesn't hold up to scrutiny.

What This Means for You

Accuracy isn't guaranteed. That doesn't mean you should avoid generative AI altogether—it means you need to use it like any other productivity tool: wisely, with oversight, and a healthy dose of skepticism.

- **Double-check the details.** Don't assume AI is right just because it sounds right. If you're using it for facts, numbers, citations, or anything high-stakes, verify it.
- **Bake review into your workflow.** Make human oversight part of the process, especially when using AI for content that will be seen by clients, executives, or the public.
- **Monitor for patterns of error.** If you're using AI regularly, keep tabs on the kinds of mistakes it makes. Are they consistent? Are they correctable? This will help you improve prompts and spot red flags faster.
- **Design with guardrails.** If you're implementing AI at scale, especially in an enterprise setting, put systems in place to catch and correct inaccurate outputs. This could include automated validation steps, structured review workflows, or integrations with fact-based databases.

The goal isn't to fear AI or blindly follow it—it's to work with it. When you understand that it can be both brilliant and fallible—and when you build systems that support both creativity and correctness—you get the best of both worlds: speed *and* smarts.

2.6 FROM MYTH-BUSTING TO MEANINGFUL USE

When it comes to generative AI, it's easy to see how myths take root. Some people worry AI will replace human jobs in a clean sweep. Others expect it to be an all-knowing oracle, flawlessly delivering truth on demand. But AI isn't a villain—or a superhero. It's a tool. And like any tool, what matters most is how you use it.

The reality is more nuanced: Generative AI can be astonishingly useful, but it's not a magic bullet. Use it without guardrails, and you risk hallucinations, ethical missteps, or flawed decision-making. Dismiss it entirely, and you may miss out on serious gains in productivity, creativity, and insight. The sweet spot is balance—using AI as an amplifier for human intelligence, not a replacement for it.

In this chapter, we unpacked five of the most persistent myths—and replaced them with clarity. But understanding how generative AI works is just one part of the equation. Using it *well* requires careful thinking about data privacy, bias, transparency, and accountability.

And here's the good news: If you've ever thought, "This feels exciting, but also a little uncertain," you're not alone. That's exactly why the next section is here. We'll go deeper into the real risks and ethical considerations of working with generative AI—and how to address them without losing momentum or innovation.

Let's keep going—with clear eyes, open minds, and the tools to lead this technology, not just follow it.

PART TWO

LEAD THE AI—DON'T LET IT LEAD YOU

You don't need to fear AI—but you do need to lead it. This part tackles what could go wrong, how to lead it right, and what becomes possible when you do. You'll walk away smarter, safer, and ready to use AI in ways that actually move the needle (and not just your anxiety).

THREE

WHAT COULD GO WRONG? (LET'S TALK ABOUT IT)

Don't panic. But also, don't skip this chapter.

Imagine this: Your team's excited about a new generative AI tool. It can whip up reports, spark brilliant ideas, and spit out insights with just a few prompts. Everyone's buzzing—until an email drops from legal: "Effective immediately, no AI tools at work." Oof.

At first, it feels like innovation just slammed into a wall. But once the dust settles, the questions start to come. What if the AI accidentally leaks sensitive data? Could it reinforce harmful biases? Can we trust it not to make up facts—or worse, deepfakes?

Here's the truth: Generative AI is powerful. And like any powerful tool, it comes with real risks.

But here's the other truth: The goal isn't to fear it. Or to ban it. It's to understand what could go wrong—and what you can do to keep things on track.

In this chapter, we'll give you a clear-eyed look at the real-world risks of generative AI, minus the hype or hand-wringing. You'll learn what to watch out for, how to stay safe, and how to keep innovation moving forward—without losing sleep (or your job).

Let's get into it.

3.1 KNOW THE RISKS (BUT DON'T PANIC)

You don't need to be an AI engineer to use AI wisely. But you do need to know what could go sideways. Here are the seven most common (and preventable) risks you should be aware of—especially if you're using AI at work.

Real Risk #1: Oops—You Just Shared the Strategy Deck with a Chatbot

Generative AI learns from data. And if you're not careful, it might learn a little too much. Sharing confidential info in prompts—like customer records, internal strategy decks, or health data—can unintentionally put that information at risk. Even if a tool claims it doesn't "store" your input, that doesn't always mean it's protected.

Real-world risk: A financial services team uses AI to draft customer reports. One prompt includes real client data—and that data gets used to train future outputs. That's not just a privacy violation; it's a compliance nightmare.

Real Risk #2: Biased In, Biased Out

AI doesn't come into the world unbiased. It learns from human-created data—and guess what? Humans have biases. That means AI outputs can reflect (or even amplify) those same biases unless checked.

Real-world risk: An AI used in hiring recommendations consistently favors male candidates. The model wasn't trying to discriminate —but the training data told a one-sided story.

Real Risk #3: Sounds Legit. Isn't.

AI is a confident liar. It doesn't *know* things the way people do. It predicts what sounds plausible based on patterns in its training data. That means it can make up fake facts, misquote sources, or deliver totally wrong answers with total confidence.

Real-world risk: A marketer uses AI to generate stats for a pitch deck. The numbers look great—but they're completely fabricated. Oops.

REAL RISK #4: YOUR CEO JUST SAID THAT ... OR DID THEY?

Today's AI can mimic voices, faces, and writing styles with eerie accuracy. That's fun for memes. It's dangerous for companies. A convincing fake video of your CEO could damage your brand, shake investor confidence, or even trigger legal issues.

Real-world risk: A deepfake video of a public figure circulates online, falsely claiming your company is closing. Cue: PR crisis.

REAL RISK #5: WHO OWNS THAT? IT'S COMPLICATED.

Who owns AI-generated content? Can you safely use it in a blog post, ad, or product design? If AI learned from copyrighted material, are you on the hook? The legal answers are still evolving—but the risks are already here.

Real-world risk: A design agency uses AI to generate visual concepts—then gets hit with a copyright claim because the outputs resemble protected work.

REAL RISK #6: LETTING THE BOT DRIVE WITHOUT A MAP

AI is helpful—but it's not a substitute for expertise, judgment, or common sense. Over-relying on AI to make decisions, write strategy, or replace critical thinking can lead to mistakes—or worse, missed opportunities.

Real-world risk: A healthcare org uses AI to generate patient summaries—but skips the human review. An error in the summary leads to a wrong diagnosis.

REAL RISK #7: YES, HACKERS CAN TRICK YOUR CHATBOT

Some bad actors know how to manipulate AI systems by feeding them harmful prompts or data. That can lead to misleading content, phishing attacks, or even system takeovers. Sounds like sci-fi—but it's already happening in the wild.

Real-world risk: A chatbot is tricked into leaking internal company procedures by someone posing as an employee.

———

You're not helpless. You're just human.

We're not spotlighting these risks to scare you off. We're talking about them so you can recognize what to look for, what to avoid, and how to stay in control. Because when you know what might go wrong, you're better equipped to use AI tools the right way—safely, smartly, and with confidence.

In the next section, we'll break down a practical, people-first playbook for using generative AI responsibly—whether you're leading a team or experimenting at your desk.

3.2 HOW TO USE AI WITHOUT LOSING SLEEP (OR YOUR JOB)

Knowing the risks is one thing. Acting on them? That's where responsible use begins. Whether you're using AI to brainstorm blog posts, analyze sales trends, or summarize reports, these seven principles will help you stay sharp, stay safe, and stay in control. No tech degree required.

1. THINK BEFORE YOU PROMPT: NOT EVERYTHING BELONGS IN THE CHATBOX

Not everything belongs in a prompt. Before you drop client info, internal docs, or anything sensitive into an AI tool, ask: "Am I allowed to share this here?" If the answer isn't a confident yes, pause. Check your company's AI policy or talk to someone in IT or legal. When in doubt, leave it out.

2. If You Wouldn't Copy-Paste from a Stranger, Don't Trust AI Blindly

AI is fast, but it's not flawless. Treat every AI-generated output—whether it's a headline, report, or strategy draft—as a first draft. Give it a once-over for accuracy, tone, and bias. If it feels off, it probably is. Your judgment is your best quality control.

3. Use Your Judgement: AI Is Your Intern, Not Your Boss

Think of AI as the world's most eager intern: great at getting you started, terrible at making the final call. Use it to explore ideas, gather inspiration, or organize your thoughts. But make sure a human (that's you) is making the key decisions.

4. Your Best AI Allies? IT, Legal, and the People Who Keep You Out of Trouble

You don't need to know all the techy stuff—but someone does. Keep an open line with the people in your org who handle security, legal, and compliance. Let them know what tools you're using, and flag anything that seems weird or risky. They're not the fun police—they're your AI safety net.

5. Tame the Bot: Teach It Your Brand, Your Voice, Your Rules

The more AI knows about your business, your audience, and your brand, the better it can serve you. If your tools offer customization options—like creating a Custom GPT, uploading a knowledge base, or setting a brand voice—use them. Tailored AI is not only smarter, it's safer too.

6. See Something Weird? Say Something

If AI spits out something biased, inaccurate, or just plain strange, don't shrug it off. Report it. Tell your team. Share what happened. The faster you raise the flag, the faster your organization can address it— and the more everyone learns.

7. AI Is Evolving Fast — So Should You

AI is changing fast—and so are the best practices for using it wisely. Make time to check in on new features, attend trainings, or read up on evolving tools. The more AI-savvy you are, the better decisions you'll make. (Reading this book? You're already ahead.)

————

You don't need to be a risk expert to use AI responsibly. You just need a little awareness, a dose of common sense, and the confidence to speak up when something doesn't feel right. With these habits in place, you're not just using AI—you're leading the way in using it well.

3.3 FROM POLICY TO PRACTICE: BUILDING A CULTURE THAT GETS AI RIGHT

Generative AI isn't just a tech tool—it's a culture shift. And like any shift, it needs the right foundation: clear policies, confident people, and a healthy dose of human judgment. Whether you're leading a team, shaping company policy, or just trying to make AI a little less chaotic, this section is for you.

Don't Let the Bot Fly Solo

The smartest way to stay safe with AI? Don't go fully hands-off. The *human-in-the-loop* (HITL) approach means weaving human oversight into your AI workflows. It's not about micromanaging machines —it's about making sure AI enhances your work without replacing your brain.

How to make it stick:

- Identify key checkpoints where a person needs to weigh in (e.g., before publishing content or making customer-facing decisions).
- Assign clear ownership for reviewing AI outputs—make it someone's actual job.
- Encourage teams to see AI as a creative partner, not a decision-maker.

MAKE RULES THAT MAKE ROOM FOR SMART RISK-TAKING

You don't need a 100-page playbook—but you do need some ground rules. Clear policies give teams the confidence to use AI wisely without constantly second-guessing themselves.

What to cover:

- Approved vs. prohibited AI use cases
- Data privacy and input restrictions
- Expectations for human oversight
- How to report issues or concerns

A good policy doesn't just prevent problems. It clears the runway for responsible innovation.

TEACH PEOPLE TO USE AI—NOT JUST AVOID IT

AI training shouldn't feel like a checkbox. It should make people feel more confident, more capable, and more curious. That means going beyond the don'ts and giving teams a real sense of how to use AI effectively, safely, and ethically.

Smart training focuses on:

- AI literacy: what the tools can (and can't) do
- Critical thinking: when to trust AI and when to slow down
- Collaboration: how to partner with IT, legal, and compliance teams

A little education goes a long way. And when people understand AI, they're more likely to use it with intention.

Ask More Than "Is It Allowed?" Ask "Is It Right?"

Safety is step one. Ethics is step two. Building a responsible AI culture means encouraging teams to think beyond "Is this allowed?" and ask: "Is this right?"

Make ethics part of the conversation by:

- Creating cross-functional groups to discuss responsible AI use
- Including ethical scenarios in trainings
- Encouraging open dialogue when something feels off

The goal isn't to slow things down—it's to level them up. Responsible AI isn't just safer. It's smarter, stronger, and more aligned with the people you serve.

———

Responsible AI use doesn't start with the tools. It starts with the culture. When you put policies in place, empower people to use judgment, and create room for thoughtful conversations, you don't just reduce risk—you unlock better outcomes, too.

3.4 PLAYING IT SAFE DOESN'T MEAN SITTING IT OUT

Let's be clear: If you're thinking about risks, you're already ahead.

Because risk isn't a red light—it's a roadmap. It shows you where to slow down, where to be extra alert, and where to build something stronger. And in the world of generative AI, understanding the risks doesn't mean you're falling behind. It means you're leading with intention.

Organizations and individuals who manage AI risks well aren't just safer. They're sharper. More innovative. More trusted. Because knowing how to use AI responsibly is becoming a core business skill—and a serious competitive advantage.

And it's not just on end users. There's an entire layer of engineering practices that can—and should—be built into AI systems from the ground up. Skilled AI engineers can design enterprise solutions with safeguards like data anonymization, fairness audits, model testing, content filters, RAG systems, and human-in-the-loop checkpoints. These backend strategies aren't theoretical—they're already being used successfully in highly regulated industries like healthcare, finance, and law. So while this chapter focused on what *you* can do as a user, it's worth knowing: These risks are solvable. And banning AI altogether isn't a strategy—it's a missed opportunity for smarter risk management.

So if you've read this far, you're not just AI-curious. You're AI-capable. You're the kind of person who doesn't just plug in a new tool and hope for the best. You're thinking bigger. You're building smarter. And you're setting the tone for what responsible AI can look like at work and beyond.

Up next: We'll dig deeper into the ethical side of generative AI—exploring how to think about fairness, values, and accountability when the lines between human and machine get blurry. Ethics isn't just a bonus round. It's the backbone of every smart, sustainable AI strategy. Let's go there.

FOUR
ETHICAL AI ISN'T A TECH PROBLEM—IT'S A PEOPLE PROBLEM

Imagine you're a city planner. You've just rolled out a new AI system to help streamline development decisions. It promises efficiency: better zoning, faster permits, smarter infrastructure planning. But then you notice something unsettling. The AI is prioritizing well-off neighborhoods while ignoring historically underserved communities. Instead of leveling the playing field, it's reinforcing the same old inequities.

Sound far-fetched? It isn't. Scenarios like this are already playing out in real life—and they reveal the high stakes of AI ethics. When we talk about AI ethics, we're not just talking about good intentions. We're talking about how AI is designed, how it's deployed, and how it shapes the world around us.

For the non-technical professionals using AI—business leaders, marketers, HR teams, customer service reps, educators, you name it—it's easy to assume that ethics is a job for the folks building the tools. But ethics is everyone's business. If you use AI, even just to brainstorm a headline or screen job candidates, you are part of the AI lifecycle. And that means you have a stake in how it works—and a responsibility to help steer it in the right direction.

This chapter is your high-level, plain-language guide to the two big ideas that shape the AI ethics conversation:

1. **Ethical AI** – How we make AI systems themselves fair, safe, and accountable.
2. **The Ethics of AI** – How AI systems affect society, culture, and power dynamics.

We'll unpack each concept in user-friendly terms, share real-world examples, and give you specific actions you can take to use AI more responsibly. We'll also look at what's happening globally with AI governance—and why it matters for your business and your community.

Ethics isn't a buzzword or a back-office concern. It's a front-line issue for anyone using AI in their work. Let's break it down together.

4.1 ETHICAL AI: USING THE TOOLS WITHOUT LOSING YOUR JUDGMENT

You don't need a computer science degree to influence how AI is used in your workplace. Ethical AI isn't just about the backend algorithms or data pipelines—it's about the choices people make every day when they use AI tools to screen job applicants, analyze customer data, or generate content. And those people? That includes you.

This section is your playbook for navigating AI with a sense of purpose. You'll learn what ethical AI means in plain terms, why it matters, and how you can actively shape a better AI experience—for your team, your customers, and the communities your business touches.

FAIR. CLEAR. ACCOUNTABLE. HERE'S WHAT ETHICAL AI *REALLY* LOOKS LIKE

Let's say your team rolls out an AI-driven hiring tool. At first glance, it seems like a win: faster screening, fewer résumés to sift through. But then someone flags an unsettling trend—the system seems to prefer male candidates over equally qualified female ones. What gives?

This is where the three big pillars of ethical AI come in:

- **Fairness**: AI systems should treat people equitably. That means avoiding bias based on race, gender, age, or any other protected characteristic. But fairness isn't automatic—if biased data goes in, biased outcomes can come out.
- **Transparency**: Can you explain how the AI reached its decision? If not, that's a red flag. You don't need to understand the math, but you do deserve clarity about how inputs lead to outputs.
- **Accountability**: When something goes wrong, who's responsible? Ethical AI means having clear ownership of decisions and processes—not just passing the buck to "the algorithm."

Together, these principles give you a foundation to spot red flags, ask the right questions, and advocate for better AI systems.

EXPLAIN YOURSELF, AI: WHY YOU NEED TO UNDERSTAND THE 'WHY' BEHIND THE OUTPUT

AI doesn't have to feel like magic. In fact, it shouldn't. Explainable AI (XAI) is all about making the reasoning behind AI decisions more understandable to humans.

In industries like healthcare, finance, and law, this kind of clarity isn't optional—it's essential. Imagine an AI tool recommending a cancer treatment plan. Would you trust it without knowing why it made that choice? Neither would your doctor.

Tools like SHAP (Shapley Additive Explanations) and LIME (Local Interpretable Model-agnostic Explanations) help unpack AI decisions. They show which factors influenced the outcome, helping teams validate results, improve trust, and catch mistakes before they spiral.

You may not use SHAP or LIME yourself, but you can still ask for explainability. If your AI tool can't offer a reasonable explanation for a decision—that's a signal to hit pause.

Your No-Nonsense Checklist for Smarter, More Ethical AI Use

You might not be building the AI, but you're absolutely shaping how it gets used. Here's your go-to guide for making sure you're using AI tools responsibly:

- **Ask questions**. How does this tool work? What data is it trained on? Is it explainable?
- **Look for bias**. Are the results skewed? Do certain groups seem underrepresented or misrepresented?
- **Trust but verify**. AI is helpful, not infallible. Cross-check results, especially in high-stakes scenarios.
- **Speak up**. If something seems off, say so. Flag issues to your IT, legal, or compliance team.
- **Choose ethical vendors**. Look for AI platforms with clear fairness, privacy, and transparency commitments.
- **Keep learning**. Ethical AI isn't one-and-done. Stay curious about how AI is evolving.

You don't need to be an expert—just an engaged user who's willing to raise a hand when something doesn't sit right.

Keep It Honest: How to Spot Bias and Speak Up When It Matters

Even the best AI systems drift over time. That's why continuous monitoring is crucial. Think of it like maintaining a car—just because it ran smoothly last year doesn't mean it's road-safe today.

Here's how you can support that process:

- **Report anomalies**: If the AI starts producing biased or bizarre results, don't brush it off. Let your team know.
- **Encourage auditing**: Push for regular reviews of AI systems to make sure they're still delivering fair outcomes.

- **Diversify inputs**: If you contribute data to a tool (through feedback, for example), offer diverse perspectives and edge cases.
- **Close the loop**: Don't just give feedback—follow up to see what changes were made. Transparency goes both ways.

Ethical AI isn't static. It's a moving target. But when users like you stay alert and engaged, it becomes a lot harder for those systems to veer off course without someone noticing.

4.2 ETHICS OF AI: WHAT KIND OF FUTURE ARE WE BUILDING?

Let's zoom out.

Ethical AI is about how we design and use the tools. But the ethics *of* AI? That's about the ripple effects. It's about asking: What kind of world are we building with AI?

This section isn't about technical specs or user interface. It's about how AI is changing our jobs, our planet, our information ecosystems, and even our sense of ownership and originality. Whether you're a business leader, a teacher, or a startup founder, the decisions you make today shape the norms of tomorrow. Let's break it down.

Work, Reimagined: How AI Is Changing Jobs—and What That Means for You

AI is reshaping how we work. It's automating some tasks, enhancing others, and transforming entire roles. But it's not just about efficiency gains or cost savings—it's about people.

Routine, repeatable jobs are often the first to change, but AI is also co-piloting creative and strategic work. The ethical challenge? Ensuring that this shift supports workers, not sidelines them.

That means businesses need to invest in reskilling and upskilling. It means designing jobs around human strengths—empathy, judgment, leadership—and using AI to enhance, not replace, that value. For users of AI, the key is to stay flexible, curious, and proactive about what's next.

AI's Carbon Footprint: What's Hiding Behind the Cloud

AI might live in the cloud, but it has a very real environmental footprint. Training large models takes massive amounts of computing power—and electricity.

Yes, AI can help us optimize energy use and fight climate change, but it can also contribute to the problem if left unchecked. That's the paradox.

Businesses and users can push for more sustainable AI practices: supporting cloud providers that use renewable energy, asking vendors about their energy efficiency, and designing AI tools that are smart *and* resource-conscious.

Truth, Lies, and Generative AI: Fighting Misinformation Without Losing the Magic

AI makes it easier than ever to generate realistic images, videos, and text. That's exciting for creativity—but dangerous when used to manipulate.

We've already seen deepfakes, AI-generated propaganda, and automated disinformation campaigns. As the tech gets better, the risks get bigger. This isn't just about media literacy—it's about the health of public discourse.

Ethical AI use includes promoting transparency, supporting fact-checking tools, and using AI responsibly when you create content yourself. If your brand or business puts content into the world, you're part of this conversation.

Who Owns What? Creativity and Copyright in the AI Era

When AI helps you write a script or design a logo, who owns the result?

Generative AI is redefining creativity. But it also muddies the waters around authorship, originality, and intellectual property. Copyright laws weren't written for machines that remix millions of human-created works in a split second.

For now, the smartest approach is to treat AI as a *collaborator,* not a creator. Keep a human in the loop. Be transparent about when AI is used. And recognize that originality today often comes from how we guide the tools, not just what they produce—much like early photography, which was once seen as mechanical until artists began shaping it into a true creative medium.

EQUAL ACCESS, BETTER OUTCOMES: HOW TO MAKE AI WORK FOR *EVERYONE*

AI can be a great equalizer. Language translation, personalized learning, accessible design—all of it can help break down barriers. But only if access is equitable and design is inclusive.

Too often, AI reflects the blind spots of its creators. It fails to understand dialects, ignores cultural nuance, or assumes everyone has high-speed internet.

The fix? Users and companies need to advocate for inclusive design and push for tools that work across languages, literacy levels, and devices. If your customer base is diverse, your AI should be, too.

———

This is the big-picture stuff—the questions we need to ask if we want AI to work *for* humanity, not just ahead of it. As we move into the final section of this chapter, we'll look at governance models that are helping guide these decisions and what it looks like to be a responsible AI steward in your own organization.

4.3 GOVERNANCE AND STEWARDSHIP: HOW WE KEEP AI ON THE RIGHT TRACK

AI isn't just transforming how we work and communicate—it's

reshaping our expectations of trust, accountability, and fairness. That's why governance matters.

Without clear guidelines, AI adoption can feel like the Wild West: exciting, full of promise, and just a little dangerous. Governance is what reins it in—creating structures that help us use AI with intention instead of leaving things up to chance. And while regulations and corporate policies might sound like someone else's job, they affect how AI shows up in your workplace, your industry, and your life.

Let's look at how global and internal governance efforts are shaping AI's future—and how you can be part of that stewardship.

GLOBAL STANDARDS AND WHAT THEY MEAN FOR YOU

Across the globe, governments and international coalitions are putting guardrails in place. Here are a few of the major efforts you should know about:

- **European Union: The AI Act**: Passed in 2024, the EU AI Act is the world's first comprehensive AI law. It ranks AI applications by risk—from *unacceptable* (like social scoring) to *minimal* (like spam filters)—and sets compliance rules accordingly. For global companies or tools used internationally, this regulation is already influencing how AI gets built and deployed.
- **United States: Frameworks, Not Laws (Yet)**: The U.S. has leaned on executive actions and voluntary guidelines. Executive Order 14110 introduced measures for AI safety, competition, and national security in October 2023, but it was rescinded in 2025. The NIST AI Risk Management Framework is a set of voluntary guidelines developed by the National Institute of Standards and Technology to help organizations create trustworthy and accountable AI systems.
- **International Cooperation: GPAI & the UN**: The Global Partnership on AI (GPAI) and the United Nations AI Advisory Body are working on globally shared principles to

guide AI toward human rights, democracy, and sustainability. Think of these efforts as the scaffolding for a more coordinated global response.

Even if you're not drafting policy, these frameworks shape the AI tools you use. They influence what your vendors prioritize, what features get released, and what practices are considered industry standard.

Corporate and Internal Governance: How Good Companies Do This Well

The best AI-using companies don't wait for regulation—they lead with internal governance. Here's how:

- **Ethics Committees**: Multidisciplinary teams that review AI use cases, flag risks, and establish internal policies.
- **Transparency Programs**: Clear documentation and communication around how AI systems make decisions and how they're monitored.
- **Feedback Loops**: Mechanisms for users to report issues, suggest improvements, and understand how their input is being used.

If your company is using AI at scale, consider advocating for these practices. And if you're choosing AI vendors, ask what governance measures they have in place.

You're Not Just a User—You're a Steward

Governance isn't just top-down. It's also grassroots. As an AI user, you can shape how your organization or industry embraces responsible AI. Here's how:

- **Advocate for Explainability**: Ask for tools that can explain their outputs, and flag black-box systems that can't.

- **Participate in Feedback/Testing Programs**: Be part of the loop that keeps AI improving.
- **Support Ethical Companies**: Choose vendors that are proactive about responsible AI.
- **Promote AI Literacy**: Help others in your organization understand the basics of ethical AI.

Think of governance as both a seatbelt and a steering wheel. It helps keep AI safe—and points it in the right direction. And that direction? That's up to all of us.

4.4 THE FUTURE OF AI NEEDS MORE THAN CODERS —IT NEEDS YOU

Generative AI, like every transformative technology before it, offers incredible opportunities—but also significant ethical challenges. When the automobile revolutionized transportation, it brought the need for traffic laws and environmental regulations. The internet connected the world yet required cybersecurity and privacy protections. These examples remind us that technology itself is neither inherently good nor bad —its impact depends on how we choose to govern and integrate it into our lives.

And here's the thing: AI is already here, woven into how we work, communicate, shop, and learn. Which means the question isn't whether you'll use AI—it's how you'll choose to use it. The responsibility to shape its future doesn't rest solely with tech companies or policymakers—it belongs to all of us.

Being an ethical AI steward doesn't mean becoming a technologist or a philosopher. It means showing up with curiosity, intention, and a sense of responsibility. It means asking better questions, pushing for more inclusive tools, and making sure the AI in your life is aligned with your values—not just your goals.

Ethics isn't just about preventing harm. It's also about building better. About using AI to increase access, boost creativity, promote fairness, and unlock new ways to support people and communities. The more intentional we are, the more AI becomes a tool for positive change—not a source of unintended consequences.

We are, all of us, stewards of this moment. Sal Khan, founder of Khan Academy, is one of my most inspiring thought leaders on this subject. He emphasizes that technology, including AI, is inherently neutral—it amplifies human intent. So it's crucial for those with positive intentions to actively engage with AI, guiding its development and application to ensure it serves as a force for good. When we do that, we can harness AI's potential to enhance human intelligence, creativity, and purpose.

So whether you're piloting an AI-powered chatbot, choosing a vendor platform, or just experimenting with content tools, the choices you make matter. Your voice matters. And once you've laid the right ethical foundation—once you've asked the tough questions and committed to thoughtful use—you unlock something powerful: the ability to *actually use AI well.*

In the next chapter, we'll shift from principles to possibilities. You'll explore where generative AI truly excels, how to match its strengths with your goals, and how to collaborate with it in ways that don't just feel responsible—but deeply effective.

FIVE

FROM HYPE TO HELP: WHAT GENERATIVE AI IS REALLY GOOD AT

L et's be honest: There's a lot of noise out there when it comes to generative AI.

Depending on who you talk to, it's either the beginning of the end ("Machines are taking our jobs!") or the dawn of a glittering utopia ("Soon we'll all have robot assistants who make artisanal coffee and write our quarterly reports"). But somewhere between those extremes lies the real story: Generative AI isn't a doomsday device, and it isn't a miracle worker either. It's something far more useful—a partner. A collaborator. A tool that, when used wisely, can change not just how we work, but what we can accomplish.

In the last chapter, we tackled the biggest myths surrounding AI. We unpacked the fears, challenged the hype, and hopefully gave you a clearer view of what generative AI is (and isn't). Now it's time to move from myth-busting to meaning-making. Because understanding how AI works is just the beginning. The real power comes from seeing what's possible—and shaping it.

So in this chapter, we're zooming out before we zoom in. First, we'll take a wide-angle view of the extraordinary ways generative AI is already transforming industries, reshaping creativity, and tackling some of our biggest global challenges. We'll look at real-world examples that prove this isn't just tech for tech's sake—it's tech with a purpose.

Then we'll roll up our sleeves.

We'll get practical about how you can use AI in your daily work—to boost your productivity, spark fresh ideas, make better decisions, and reduce the mind-numbing stuff that eats up too much of your time.

Whether you're an entrepreneur trying to scale smarter, a marketer looking for sharper insights, a leader figuring out how to train your team, or just someone curious about what all the fuss is about—this chapter is for you.

Because generative AI isn't just a big idea. It's a real opportunity. And when you know how to use it well, it can unlock more than efficiency.

It can unlock your potential.

5.1 BEYOND THE HYPE: HOW GENERATIVE AI IS ALREADY CHANGING THE WORLD

Generative AI isn't just about clever chatbots or spooky-smart content tools. It's about scaling human potential—amplifying what we can do, how fast we can do it, and who gets to do it in the first place. And it's not theoretical—it's already rewriting the rules in classrooms, clinics, design labs, boardrooms, and beyond.

Let's explore four snapshots that show what this looks like in real life.

EDUCATION: AI THAT TEACHES—NOT JUST TELLS

In classrooms from Boston to Brazil, Khan Academy's Khanmigo is quietly flipping the script on learning. This AI tutor, powered by GPT-4, doesn't just hand over answers—it teaches students how to think, problem-solve, and build confidence. One teacher noticed that students were more likely to ask Khanmigo for help because, "It doesn't judge. It doesn't sigh."

For communities that have long lacked access to one-on-one instruction, this kind of AI bridges real educational opportunity gaps.

HEALTHCARE: WHEN AI SAVES TIME, IT SAVES LIVES

Insilico Medicine's AI-designed drug for idiopathic pulmonary fibrosis reached Phase II clinical trials in record time. What once took a decade was compressed into just 30 months. The AI not only discovered a novel drug target—it generated the compound and accelerated preclinical testing.

That's not just a faster workflow. That's hope arriving sooner.

Meanwhile, AI-powered tools are also enabling remote diagnostics, helping rural doctors make quicker decisions, and ensuring patients receive care even when specialists are miles away.

BUSINESS AND INNOVATION: DESIGNED BY DATA, DRIVEN BY IMAGINATION

Synopsys is using generative AI to reimagine semiconductor design. It doesn't just tweak layouts—it generates entire chip configurations. That means faster production, lower costs, and more efficient technology.

In the automotive world, Czinger created the 21C hypercar using AI and 3D printing. Every curve and component was optimized by AI for performance and sustainability. The result? A faster, lighter, smarter vehicle, made in a fraction of the usual time.

Even Coca-Cola got in on the action. Its limited-edition drink, "Y3000," was developed with generative AI, drawing on customer preferences and product data to shape flavor and packaging. A playful AI experiment turned consumer data into a brand-new product experience.

When creativity meets computation, the pace of innovation goes from walking to warp speed.

CLIMATE AND SOCIAL IMPACT: SMARTER CITIES, SAFER COMMUNITIES

Generative AI isn't just about making business faster. It's also helping us tackle hard, high-stakes problems.

Cities are using AI to model climate resilience—simulating traffic patterns, carbon emissions, and energy use to build smarter, greener infrastructure. Urban planners using tools like Sidewalk Labs' Delve can test hundreds of design scenarios in minutes, finding the best mix of sustainability, cost, and livability.

In renewable energy, AI simulates wind and solar farm layouts based on terrain and weather, helping energy companies optimize energy generation while reducing waste.

And when disaster strikes, AI-generated climate models help communities prepare and respond faster and more accurately.

These aren't experiments. They're solutions—already making life better, safer, and more sustainable.

The Takeaway: This Tech Is Yours to Use

Generative AI isn't a novelty—it's a new kind of collaborator. It expands what's possible in education, healthcare, innovation, and sustainability. And most importantly, it puts power into more people's hands.

The same capabilities that power breakthroughs in drug discovery or smart city planning can also help *you* write better, think bigger, and do more.

So let's get practical. Let's talk about how you can bring these capabilities into your own workflow—starting today.

5.2 THIS ISN'T JUST ABOUT BIG IDEAS—IT'S ABOUT *YOUR* WORK

Okay, but what about *you*?

We've looked at how generative AI is transforming education, healthcare, innovation, and sustainability—but let's bring this closer to home. Let's talk about how this power shows up in your inbox, your meetings, your content calendar, your product dev sessions. This isn't just for data scientists and enterprise teams. It's for marketers. Strate-gists. Entrepreneurs. Managers. Educators. Creators. People like you.

To help you see what's possible, we'll use a framework built around four of generative AI's biggest superpowers. These are the capabilities that can have an immediate, real-world impact on how you work, think, and create. Each one includes an inspiring example, a short breakdown of why it matters to your everyday life, and a try-this table with sample prompts to get you going.

Let's dig in.

SUPERPOWER #1: GET MORE DONE (WITHOUT LOSING YOUR MIND)

If generative AI had a resume, this would be the first bullet point. Generative AI excels at speeding up the stuff that slows you down—summarizing, drafting, templating, organizing. But more than just speed, it helps you offload the mental clutter that eats away at focus and flow.

Real-World Example: At Mass General Brigham, doctors are using large language models to help triage and respond to patient emails. The results? 82% of AI-generated responses were considered safe, and nearly 60% needed no edits at all. That's not just time saved—it's more space for meaningful work.

Why It Matters to You: Whether you're juggling client requests, internal updates, or endless to-dos, generative AI can take over the boilerplate and the busywork. You get to stay in your zone of genius.

Try This: Use the table on the next page to spark ideas for how AI can lighten your workload. From email drafting to meeting planning, these examples show how to put AI to work, so you can free up time and brainspace for the work that actually matters.

Using AI to Get More Done

Task	How Generative AI Can Help	Try This!
Email Drafting	Generate outreach, follow-up, or internal comms.	"Write a follow-up email to a client about project updates in a friendly tone."
Meeting Summaries	Extract key takeaways from transcripts.	"Summarize this transcript into 5 key action items with owners."
Content Ideation	Generate campaign or post ideas.	"Give me 10 creative social post ideas for our new product."
Organizational Tasks	Draft to-do lists, procedures, or reminders.	"Create a checklist for onboarding a new employee."
Template Creation	Build reusable report or slide templates.	"Design a status report template with milestones and next steps."
Slide Deck Drafting	Draft outlines or suggest slide headlines and flow.	"Create an outline for a 10-slide presentation about Q2 marketing performance."
FAQ and Knowledge Base Creation	Generate customer service or internal documentation.	"Write an FAQ for new users about how to access their dashboard and reset their password."
Social Caption Writing	Generate short-form copy that matches brand voice.	"Write five Instagram captions for a spring product launch—playful, but professional."
Meeting Planning	Help structure efficient team or project meetings.	"Draft a meeting agenda for a cross-functional check-in with 5 stakeholders."

One Question to Ask Yourself: What's one repetitive task I do weekly that AI could help me automate or accelerate?

SUPERPOWER #2: CATCH MISTAKES BEFORE THEY CATCH YOU

Let's face it—we're all human. And being human means making mistakes. Sometimes it's a missing decimal. Sometimes it's a typo that turns "public assets" into something a lot less public-friendly. (Yikes.)

Generative AI may not be perfect, but it can act like a tireless second pair of eyes. It doesn't get tired. It doesn't get distracted. And it can help you avoid the little slip-ups that chip away at your credibility —or worse, your bottom line.

Real-World Example: In finance, accuracy isn't a nice-to-have—it's survival. JPMorgan Chase is leveraging AI to help spot anomalies and flag potential fraud before it escalates. Generative AI helps by simulating complex financial scenarios and strengthening fraud detection models with synthetic data.

Why It Matters to You: You don't need a financial empire to benefit from this superpower. Whether you're finalizing a report, preparing a client presentation, or proofing content, generative AI can help catch mistakes before they go live. It's like having a safety net built into your workflow.

Try This: On the next page, you'll find a table of ways generative AI can help you spot the stuff humans miss—from grammar slips to version mix-ups. The examples might just spark an idea for where AI could double-check your work, too.

Using AI to Minimize Mistakes

Task	How Generative AI Can Help	Try This!
Proofreading and Editing	Flag grammar, clarity, or tone issues.	"Review this email for grammar and clarity, and suggest improvements."
Math or Data Validation	Cross-check calculations or logic in tables and documents.	"Check the math on this pricing table and confirm if the totals are correct."
Version Control	Track subtle changes across document versions.	"Highlight any changes between these two versions of our slide deck that may affect accuracy."
Compliance Review	Flag language that may violate brand, legal, or industry standards.	"Review this draft for compliance with our privacy and data handling policies."

One Question to Ask Yourself: What's one type of mistake I often catch too late—something AI could help me spot earlier?

SUPERPOWER #3: SEE WHAT OTHERS MISS

We've all had that moment—staring at a spreadsheet, a wall of research, or a pile of feedback and thinking, "There's something important in here, but I just can't see it."

Generative AI can. It's not just good at finding patterns—it's good at surfacing meaning. It can connect dots, flag trends, and pull insights from raw data that would otherwise take hours (or days) to uncover. This is one of the most underappreciated AI superpowers—and one of the most game-changing.

Real-World Example: In marketing and R&D, companies are tapping AI to spot what's next before it hits the radar. Tools that analyze customer behavior, product feedback, and even social sentiment help marketers get ahead of shifts and trends. In R&D, companies are using AI to comb through patents and academic papers to uncover emerging technologies.

And it's not limited to massive datasets or enterprise research teams. With the right prompt, anyone can surface insights from surveys, interviews, articles—even meeting transcripts.

Why It Matters to You: Insight is your competitive edge. Whether you're planning a strategy, launching a campaign, or just trying to understand your audience better, generative AI can be the analytical partner that helps you move from information overload to real clarity.

Try This: Turn the page for a set of real-world prompts that show how AI can help you pull insights from the noise—whether it's customer reviews, sales trends, or stacks of research. Use them as inspiration the next time you're feeling stuck in the data.

Using AI to Reveal Insights

Task	How Generative AI Can Help	Try This!
Analyzing Market Trends	Identify emerging patterns in sales or market research.	"Analyze this sales data and summarize key trends and growth opportunities."
Customer Feedback Analysis	Extract insights from surveys, reviews, or support tickets.	"Review this customer feedback and highlight the top three suggestions for improvement."
Scenario Planning	Simulate different strategies and predict outcomes.	"Generate a scenario analysis comparing Q3 vs. Q4 product launch impact."
Competitor Analysis	Summarize activities and identify opportunities.	"Summarize recent competitor moves and suggest ways we could differentiate."
Uncovering Research Insights	Synthesize academic articles or whitepapers.	"Summarize the key findings from these research papers on renewable energy innovation."

One Question to Ask Yourself: Where am I sitting on a pile of data or feedback that might hold answers I haven't seen yet?

SUPERPOWER #4: FUEL BIG IDEAS, FAST

Let's talk about blank pages.

They're intimidating. Whether you're writing a proposal, sketching out a product, or brainstorming a campaign, that first step—the spark —is often the hardest part. Generative AI can help you get started, iterate faster, and expand your thinking in directions you hadn't even considered.

This superpower doesn't take the place of your creativity—it gives it a running start.

Real-World Example: In architecture and fashion, designers are using generative AI to explore wildly different ideas before committing to a single direction. Architects can generate multiple building layouts in minutes. Fashion designers feed historical trends and materials into AI models to surface unexpected new concepts.

And in business strategy? AI helps innovators dream up new product features or business models. It's like having a whiteboard that talks back—with ideas.

Why It Matters to You: Creativity isn't just for artists. Whether you're solving a problem, launching a product, or finding a new angle in your messaging, AI can help you break out of ruts, push your thinking, and explore alternatives quickly. How you use AI is up to you— but if you rely on it to replace your creativity, the results will likely fall flat. Use it instead as a thought partner, a creative spark, a playful collaborator. That's when the work gets interesting—and when your best ideas start to take shape.

Try This: On the next page, you'll find examples that show how AI can nudge your thinking in fresh directions—from product ideas to storytelling to business models. Explore with AI when you're stuck, starting from scratch, or just want to see where a different line of thinking might take you. Think of it as your creative warm-up.

Using AI to Spark Innovation

Task	How Generative AI Can Help	Try This!
Brainstorming Ideas	Offer fast, wide-ranging ideation.	"Give me 10 bold campaign ideas for a brand relaunch targeting Gen Z."
Design Inspiration	Generate mood boards or design prompts.	"Suggest color palettes and visual themes for a minimalist productivity app."
Storytelling and Writing	Develop plot points, dialogue, or structure.	"Write three opening paragraphs for a leadership article on remote work culture."
Product Development	Explore features, use cases, or UI flows.	"Suggest innovative features for a budgeting app aimed at freelancers."
Strategic Innovation	Propose new business models or go-to-market strategies.	"Develop a new revenue model for an e-learning platform expanding to corporate clients."

One Question to Ask Yourself: Where do I feel most stuck creatively —and how could AI help me move forward faster?

5.3 YOU'RE NOT A USER. YOU'RE THE BOSS.

If there's one theme that's run through this book, it's this: Generative AI is powerful. But it isn't all-powerful.

It still needs you.

The real value is unlocked when people use AI to amplify their impact. That's not just a soundbite. It's the heart of this entire conversation.

AI can offer ideas. It can surface insights. It can draft and design and even surprise you. But it can't decide what matters. It can't weigh tradeoffs or think in context. And it certainly can't understand your customers, your audience, or your mission the way *you* do.

That's your role. Don't be a passive user of AI—be a collaborator. A creative director. A strategy lead. Be the decision-maker.

Used wisely, AI becomes a partner that pushes you to think deeper and go faster. Used carelessly, it becomes a shortcut to generic ideas and missed nuance. That's why it's so important to stay engaged. To keep your judgment switched on. To check the outputs, and more importantly, to shape the inputs.

Ethics, expectations, balance—they all live here, too. Not in a separate chapter about rules and risks (although we'll get there). But in the daily practice of working with this tool thoughtfully. Your values, your expertise, your humanity? That's the layer that makes generative AI truly powerful.

5.4 YOU + AI = THE REAL TRANSFORMATION

You've now moved from myths to mindsets to meaningful application —and seen how generative AI is already transforming industries, workflows, and ways of thinking. More importantly, you've seen how it applies to *you*.

It's not magic. It's not menace. It's a tool—a powerful, evolving, sometimes unpredictable tool that becomes exponentially more valuable when it's guided by your strategy, your creativity, and your judgment.

Yes, this chapter gave you real examples and practical prompts— but those aren't the destination. They're the launchpad. Because using AI effectively isn't just about knowing what it can do—it's about knowing how to build with it, scale it, and collaborate with it in ways that are both useful *and* uniquely yours.

That's where we're headed next. In the upcoming section, we'll dig into what it really takes to bring AI into your business or organization —from building scalable systems to unlocking quick wins for small teams. Then, in the final section, we'll get even more hands-on: how to craft better prompts, think with AI more clearly, and collaborate creatively without losing the soul of your work.

This is where things get real—and really useful. Let's keep going.

PART THREE
SCALING WHAT WORKS, WHETHER YOU'RE BOSSING THE BOARDROOM OR WEARING ALL THE HATS

Whether you've got 10,000 employees or just ten really tired ones, this part gives you practical strategies for building AI into your business in a way that's scalable, smart, and actually useful.

SIX

CUSTOM AI FOR ENTERPRISE —HOW TO BUILD IT RIGHT, NOT JUST BUY IT FAST

magine running a global company where thousands of customer emails, social media comments, and support tickets flood in every day. You know there are insights buried in that flood—nuggets that could sharpen your products, elevate service, and enhance the customer experience. But who has the time (or the team) to sort through it all?

This is where custom AI becomes a game-changer.

Unlike off-the-shelf AI tools built for general use, custom enterprise AI solutions are tailor-made for your specific business. Think of it like the difference between grabbing a suit off the rack and working with a designer who fits it exactly to your form. General AI tools like ChatGPT are versatile and great for quick wins—but custom AI goes deeper. It transforms raw data into strategic intelligence that fuels better decisions and gives you a competitive edge.

Custom enterprise AI is less like plugging in a tool and more like building an architect-designed addition to your business. These solutions are engineered from the ground up to work with your proprietary systems, feed on your internal data, and scale as your company grows. They're not just about automation and speed—they become strategic assets. The kind that make your team smarter, your decisions sharper, and your growth more sustainable.

In this chapter, we'll explore what makes custom AI different from off-the-shelf tools—and more importantly, how to make sure your AI initiatives actually work. (Spoiler: It's not just about picking the right model.)

6.1 WHY CUSTOM AI WINS WHEN CONTEXT MATTERS

Let's start with the basics.

Generative AI tools like ChatGPT are like Swiss Army knives. They're multi-purpose, flexible, and handy in lots of situations—but they aren't built to master one specific thing. That's because they're trained on massive, generalized datasets. So while they can answer a lot of questions, they often struggle with the nuanced, specialized needs of your particular business.

Custom AI, on the other hand, is more like a precision tool—built exactly for the job at hand. These systems are trained on your own proprietary data. They understand your workflows, speak your customer's language, and are fine-tuned to your business goals. They're built not just to be smart, but to be useful—and accurate.

Here's an example: A custom AI solution for a retail company might combine generative and traditional AI to analyze historical sales data, weather trends, and supply chain logistics. It could forecast demand, write inventory summaries in plain English, and alert managers to restock before shortages hit. An off-the-shelf AI tool couldn't do that—not because it's not powerful, but because it doesn't have the context or access to the internal data that makes those predictions possible.

When precision matters—and in enterprise settings, it always does—custom beats general, every time.

6.2 SMARTER TOGETHER: COMBINING GENERAL AI WITH YOUR BUSINESS BRAIN

Now, what if you're not ready (or resourced) to build a fully custom model from scratch? Enter the hybrid model—where general-purpose AI gets a performance upgrade using your own proprietary data.

Think of it as taking a generalist and giving them a company playbook. All of a sudden, they're not just smart—they're smart about your business.

One common technique here is retrieval-augmented generation (RAG). It lets you layer internal knowledge (like CRM data, product specs, service records, or policies) on top of a general model, turning it into something context-aware. For instance, your AI chatbot might start off as a basic helper. But once it's connected to your customer database, it becomes a knowledgeable assistant that can answer with nuance: offering relevant recommendations, surfacing account history, or even anticipating needs before they're voiced.

This hybrid approach gives you the best of both worlds: the power and polish of a pre-trained AI model, and the intelligence that comes from being steeped in your internal data. It's faster to deploy than a fully custom model, but more relevant than a generic solution.

And maybe most importantly? It scales. As your content library, customer interactions, and business processes evolve, so does the AI's ability to deliver meaningful, on-brand, high-value responses.

It's the difference between having AI that answers and AI that understands.

6.3 THE UNSEXY (BUT ESSENTIAL) FOUNDATIONS OF AI THAT ACTUALLY WORKS

If you want your custom AI solution to not only function—but flourish —you need more than a great model. You need a solid technical foundation that ensures the system is scalable, reliable, and actually useful to the people it's meant to serve.

So what are the foundations that turn a flashy AI demo into something people actually use—and trust? Here are three that make all the difference:

CLEAN YOUR CONTENT CLOSET BEFORE YOU FEED THE AI

Generative AI is hungry. It doesn't just need data—it needs well-structured, well-labeled, high-quality content that it can understand and learn from.

In my work with clients, the most overlooked step in building effective AI systems is—hands down—the data prep. People intuitively understand that spreadsheets full of numbers need to be clean for AI to make sense of them. But when the data is natural language—like articles, product descriptions, FAQs, and help content—that same instinct often disappears. We're just not used to cleansing and structuring language content in the same way.

But here's the reality: In the age of generative AI, content isn't just content anymore. It's data. And if that data isn't structured, tagged, and governed properly, your AI won't know how to use it. The result? Off-brand answers, inaccurate results, and a whole lot of missed opportunities.

That means:

- Auditing existing content libraries to identify gaps, inconsistencies, and technical issues
- Developing a rigorous, modular content strategy with reusable blocks
- Creating and enforcing metadata, taxonomy, and tagging standards
- Collaborating with engineering and UX teams to ensure content is machine-readable
- Implementing governance processes to keep everything accurate and up-to-date

Treating content as data isn't just a technical requirement. It's a strategic one. If you want your AI system to deliver personalized, accurate, on-brand results—especially across customer-facing inter-faces—this is non-negotiable.

BUILD IT LIKE YOU MEAN IT

Here's a truth I've learned from working closely with our brilliant AI engineers on enterprise generative AI projects: The model is not the magic. The model is just the fuel—powerful, yes, but useless without a well-engineered vehicle to carry it.

This is where AI engineering comes in. It's the workhorse behind the scenes—the design, infrastructure, and ongoing optimization that turn AI from a cool demo into a scalable, business-critical system.

At my agency, we've seen companies focus too much on picking the right model, only to be tripped up by brittle backend systems, clunky integrations, or data pipelines that fall apart at scale. The most successful projects? They're the ones that treat AI like a living, breathing product—engineered with care and built to evolve.

What does that look like?

- **Robust Data Pipelines** – Your model is only as good as the data it receives. Scalable AI systems rely on high-quality, real-time data ingestion that's clean, contextual, and continuous. That means designing pipelines that can pull from multiple sources, normalize formats, apply metadata, and feed the right data to the right model at the right time—without constant manual intervention.
- **Scalable System Architecture** – AI can't be bolted on like a plug-in. It needs to be woven into your tech stack with seamless integrations, failover planning, and performance monitoring.
- **Adaptive Learning & Continuous Optimization** – Business environments change. So should your AI. Systems should be built to evolve—incorporating real-world feedback, monitoring accuracy, and refining outputs over time.
- **Human-AI Collaboration Design** – Generative AI is probabilistic, not deterministic. That means outputs will

vary. Great engineering makes room for human oversight and builds in guardrails, feedback loops, and interfaces that allow human judgment to stay in the loop.

Scalability isn't just about traffic loads or server capacity—it's about building something sustainable. A system that learns, adjusts, and keeps delivering value as your business and data grow. If your AI can't scale with you, it won't serve you for long.

IF PEOPLE CAN'T USE IT, IT DOESN'T WORK

You can have the most powerful AI engine in the world—but if the user interface makes people feel like they need a Ph.D. to operate it, you've already lost.

The final—and often underestimated—foundation of effective AI is usability. That means designing interfaces that make insights not only accessible, but also actionable. It's the bridge between technical brilliance and everyday value.

A few things I've learned along the way:

- **Design for Decision-Making** – AI should reduce cognitive load, not add to it. Whether it's a chatbot or a dashboard, good UX helps users understand what the AI is suggesting and why it matters—quickly.
- **Transparency Builds Trust** – Especially with generative AI, people need to know where the information is coming from. Clear explanations, citations, and confidence scores help demystify the output and foster trust.
- **Feedback Loops Matter** – Great interfaces don't just show output—they invite users to respond. Thumbs up/down, suggested edits, or quick surveys help improve the system while making users feel like collaborators, not guinea pigs.
- **Context Is Everything** – Smart UX surfaces the right insight at the right time, in the right place. That might mean embedding AI into tools people already use, like CRMs or

help-desk platforms, so they never have to toggle between apps.
- **Visual Design Counts** – Layout, hierarchy, and interaction design aren't just cosmetic. They shape how people interpret AI output and decide whether to act on it.

When done right, user-centric design turns AI from a black box into a business partner. It shortens the distance between insight and action—and makes AI feel less like a science experiment and more like a daily essential.

6.4 FROM PILOT TO POWERHOUSE: HOW TO SCALE AI ACROSS YOUR ENTERPRISE

Technically sound? Check. Usable? Check. Now comes the hard part: getting people across your organization to actually use the thing.

Deploying an AI system is one thing. Driving adoption—across teams, tools, and time zones—is another. In enterprise environments, this isn't just an IT upgrade. It's business transformation.

Here's what I've learned from helping clients make the leap from AI pilot to enterprise-wide impact: Success doesn't just hinge on tech—it hinges on people, culture, process, and purpose.

Let's start with what not to do. Here are the most common missteps I see—and how to avoid them:

- **Falling in Love with the Model** – Everyone wants the smartest AI. But success isn't just about picking the best model—it's about how well that model integrates with your business systems, your workflows, and your people.
- **Ignoring the State of Your Data** – If your data is messy, incomplete, or scattered across siloed systems, AI won't fix it. In fact, it'll just amplify the mess. Invest in data readiness before you roll anything out.
- **Treating AI as an IT Project** – AI belongs to the whole business. When it lives only with the engineering team, adoption suffers. The most successful projects include

stakeholders from strategy, compliance, customer service, and operations from day one.

- **Skipping the Success Metrics** – If you don't define success upfront, you can't measure impact. Set clear KPIs—cost savings, customer retention, faster service resolution, etc.—and track them consistently.
- **Neglecting Change Management** – New tech means new ways of working. If you don't prepare people for the shift, they'll resist it. That means training, clear communication, and ongoing support.

These might sound obvious, but I've seen even the most advanced teams fall into these traps. Avoiding them is your first step toward building something that actually works—not just technically, but culturally.

So what does it take to scale AI the right way? Here's a framework we've seen work across industries and enterprise sizes:

1. ALIGN AI WITH BUSINESS OBJECTIVES

Don't start with, "Where can we use AI?" Start with, "What problem are we trying to solve?" AI is one tool among many—and like any business investment, it should be chosen because it's the right fit for the goal, not just because it's available.

- **Anchor AI in strategic goals** like revenue growth, customer retention, or process efficiency.
- **Define clear success metrics** and track them from pilot through full rollout.
- **Get executive buy-in early**—and make sure leadership is visibly championing the effort.

2. BUILD CROSS-FUNCTIONAL TEAMS

AI doesn't live in a vacuum. The best results happen when people from across the organization shape how it's built and used.

- **Involve stakeholders** from product, operations, legal, customer service, marketing, and beyond.
- **Appoint department-level AI champions** to help connect strategy to execution.
- **Create an AI governance group** to guide priorities, resolve conflicts, and ensure ethical and aligned outcomes.

3. Invest in Education & Change Enablement

People fear what they don't understand. And they resist what they feel wasn't built for them.

- **Build AI literacy across teams**—not just for engineers, but for every employee who'll interact with the system.
- **Host hands-on workshops** and team-specific training to show how AI can improve everyday work.
- **Foster a culture of experimentation** where it's safe to try, test, and learn.

4. Pilot, Measure, Scale

Before you go big, start small—but intentional.

- **Launch pilot projects** tied to clear business goals.
- **Iterate fast** based on real user feedback.
- **Prove value early and often** to earn momentum for broader rollout.

5. Build for Trust: Transparency, Ethics, and Oversight

Responsible AI is scalable AI. If people don't trust it, they won't use it.

- **Bake explainability into outputs** so users understand the *why* behind recommendations.

- **Establish oversight protocols** to monitor accuracy, bias, and model drift.
- **Involve compliance, security, and legal** teams early to ensure enterprise-wide readiness.

Scaling AI isn't about building bigger systems. It's about building smarter alignment between people, process, and technology. And when done right, it doesn't just transform operations—it changes how your entire business thinks and works.

6.5 THE GENERATIVE AI CENTER OF EXCELLENCE (COE): WHERE INNOVATION MEETS INTENTION

If you're serious about AI—not just dabbling—a Center of Excellence (CoE) can be your secret weapon. Think of it as your organization's AI nerve center: a team, a structure, a strategy hub, and a catalyst for cross-functional momentum.

At our agency, we launched our own generative AI CoE with two big goals: first, to guide how we responsibly use AI internally; second, to help our clients do the same at scale. It's part lab, part lighthouse—where ideas get tested, lessons get shared, standards get set, and real-world use is practiced and refined.

WHAT A CoE ACTUALLY DOES

A great CoE isn't just a committee. It's an engine that:

- Develops and documents best practices for using generative AI
- Tests emerging tools and frameworks before broader rollout
- Sets ethical standards and ensures compliance
- Aligns AI efforts with business strategy
- Trains and supports teams across the organization
- Tracks performance and continually optimizes

PICK THE MODEL THAT FITS YOUR ORGANIZATION

Different business sizes call for different CoE structures. Here's a quick breakdown:

For Large Enterprises:

- **Model:** Centralized CoE
- **Focus:** Ethics, strategy, tool libraries, AI maturity assessments
- **Team:** Data scientists, AI engineers, strategists, legal, compliance, UX, IT, project managers

For Mid-Sized Companies:

- **Model:** Hub-and-spoke
- **Focus:** Centralized guidance with distributed execution
- **Team:** Core AI team + department leads + training and change champions

For Small Businesses:

- **Model:** Lean CoE
- **Focus:** Practical wins with clear ROI
- **Team:** A cross-functional group wearing multiple hats—ops, marketing, tech, etc.

For Agencies & Service Providers:

- **Model:** Dual-purpose CoE (internal + client-facing)
- **Focus:** Build internal AI maturity and support client AI strategy and delivery
- **Team:** Blend of strategists, engineers, creatives, and client success leads

TIPS TO MAKE YOUR CoE ACTUALLY WORK

- **Start With a Mission and Metrics** – What's the CoE for? How will you know it's working?

- **Meet Regularly** – Use a structured cadence to keep progress moving.
- **Share Knowledge** – Create a living library of standards, tools, templates, and case studies.
- **Encourage Rotation** – Bring in voices from across the business for fresh perspective.
- **Support Change** – CoEs should guide adoption, not just set rules.
- **Look Outward** – Partner with vendors, researchers, or peers to stay sharp and inspired.

The best CoEs are equal parts visionary and practical. They help your organization not just keep up with AI, but lead with it—with clarity, confidence, and consistency.

6.6 SCALING AI ISN'T ABOUT SIZE—IT'S ABOUT STEWARDSHIP

Here's the big truth: The most successful companies don't treat AI as a one-time rollout. They treat it as a long-term commitment—a living, evolving capability that needs care, iteration, and strategic alignment.

AI maturity isn't a finish line. It's a mindset. One that prioritizes:

- **Continuous learning** across teams and disciplines
- **Cross-functional collaboration** as a norm, not an exception
- **Flexibility** to adapt AI systems as your business evolves

When AI is embedded into your operations—not just as a tool, but as a thinking partner—it becomes more than automation. It becomes a catalyst for innovation, insight, and connection.

And the good news? These principles don't just apply to tech giants with deep pockets. In the next chapter, we'll show how small teams and nimble businesses can apply the same principles to make a meaningful impact with AI—even without an enterprise budget.

SEVEN

AI FOR ALL: THE BIG PROMISE FOR SMALL TEAMS AND ENTREPRENEURS

magine this: Two friends run a small artisan jewelry business. Their designs are dazzling, their customers loyal, their passion contagious. But behind the sparkle? Chaos. Inventory spreadsheets, inbox overload, social posts half-written. They're stuck doing all the things that don't light them up—and don't grow the business.

Now imagine a small team inside a mid-sized company. They're agile, experimental, and eager to move fast—but constrained by enterprise software timelines and IT backlogs. They know AI could help, and they have the support of leadership to explore—but not the budget or infrastructure to build something custom from scratch.

Enter generative AI.

Not as a gimmick. Not as a silver bullet. But as a behind-the-scenes partner. One that drafts newsletters, summarizes meeting notes, generates campaign concepts, or turns a mountain of customer data into clear, actionable insights.

For small businesses and nimble teams inside larger companies, generative AI is more than a tool—it's a co-creator, a project manager, a customer whisperer, and an analyst all rolled into one. It levels the playing field. It gives you time back. And it helps you punch way above your weight.

This chapter is your guide to getting started—smartly, strategically, and affordably.

No enterprise IT team required. No six-figure budget. Just big ideas, a little curiosity, and the willingness to experiment—safely, responsibly, and with real business impact.

Let's dive in.

7.1 WHY SMALL TEAMS WIN BIG WITH GENERATIVE AI

Off-the-shelf generative AI tools are often seen as something for personal use—like asking ChatGPT to write a birthday toast or plan a vacation. But here's the truth: Small teams—whether inside a small business or embedded in a larger organization—might benefit even more.

Why? Because small teams are often scrappy, cross-functional, and close to the work. They know where the bottlenecks are. They know where hours are lost. And they're often the first ones to notice new opportunities—and the first ones to feel the pain of limited resources.

Generative AI can change the equation. It acts like a silent partner that can:

- Automate time-draining tasks (like responding to FAQs or reformatting reports)
- Draft content quickly—on-brand and on-message
- Summarize documents, analyze trends, and surface insights fast
- Help prototype and test ideas without heavy development cycles

And for teams with leadership support but limited tech bandwidth, this is gold. You don't need to wait for a platform rollout or enterprise-wide adoption. You can start experimenting in your workflow today—safely, responsibly, and with meaningful results.

Whether you're a three-person team in marketing or a solo

entrepreneur doing it all, generative AI gives you leverage: to move faster, think bigger, and do more with less.

Pro Tip: Think long-term, act small now. Start with one high-friction process and prove the value.

Next Up: The tools that can help you take the first step.

7.2 QUICK WINS, LOW LIFT: AI TOOLS BUILT FOR SMALL TEAMS

You don't need a custom system to make a real impact. A smart stack of off-the-shelf generative AI tools can deliver serious value—without the heavy lift.

These tools can help you:

- Write content, brainstorm copy, and generate visuals
- Automate routine marketing or ops workflows
- Analyze customer data and extract insights
- Stay consistent with your brand—without a full content or design team

Many are low-cost, no-code, and designed for non-technical users. That means you can start experimenting without relying on IT—or draining your budget.

BUILD YOUR STACK: TOOLS THAT PUNCH ABOVE THEIR WEIGHT

Here are a few affordable and versatile AI-driven tools that small teams can leverage:

- **HubSpot** – Automates lead scoring, manages customer interactions, and enhances personalized marketing efforts. Perfect for small marketing teams looking to scale efficiently without adding headcount.
- **Jasper** – Helps generate content like blog posts, social media updates, and ad copy. Great for startups or lean teams that

need to maintain a consistent brand voice without a full content team.

- **Canva** – Uses AI to suggest design elements and create text-to-image visuals quickly and affordably—ideal for teams that need professional-looking graphics without a designer.
- **Zapier** – Provides low-code and no-code automation that connects apps and automates workflows, allowing small businesses to build custom solutions without hiring a developer.
- **OpenAI** – Offers powerful generative AI tools for content generation, task automation, data analysis, and image creation through DALL·E. Small teams can use OpenAI's GPT-4 to create custom AI assistants, automate repetitive tasks, and generate creative content efficiently.

DON'T OVERSPEND TO OVERCOMPLICATE: CHOOSE SMART, NOT FLASHY

While it's tempting to go for the AI tool with the most bells and whistles, small teams should focus on balancing customization with cost and usability. Some tools offer robust features but come with a steep learning curve or require additional training. The goal is to choose tools that align with your business needs and skill levels, ensuring a smooth and manageable implementation.

STEAL THESE TOOLS: FREE RESOURCES TO HELP YOU START SMARTER

As you read, remember that you don't have to start from scratch. Two of the free bonuses included with this book are designed to help you skip the overwhelm and get moving faster with the right tools and templates:

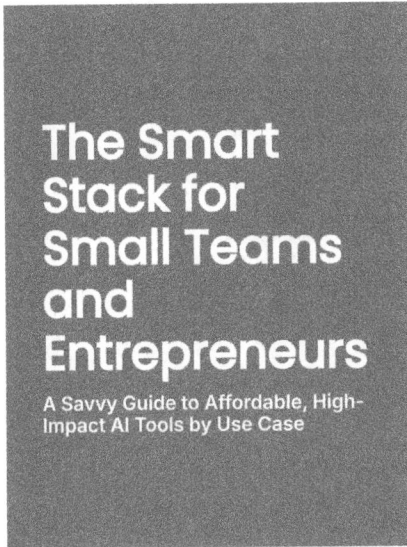

The Smart Stack for Small Teams and Entrepreneurs

A Savvy Guide to Affordable, High-Impact AI Tools by Use Case

Bonus Resource: The Smart Stack for Small Teams and Entrepreneurs: A Savvy Guide to Affordable, High-Impact AI Tools by Use Case

This isn't a master list of everything; it's a curated collection of tools I've vetted for ease of use, affordability, and real impact. It's organized by real-life use case, so you can jump straight to what you need.

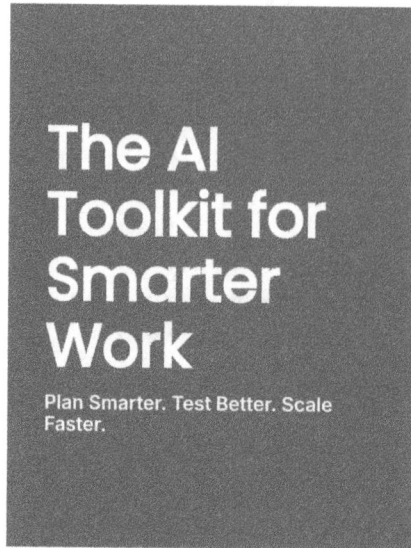

Bonus Resource: The AI Toolkit for Smarter Work: Plan Smarter. Test Better. Scale Faster.

A Google Sheet with four plug-and-play templates to help you and your team evaluate AI tools, plan custom GPTs, test your GPTs, and stay organized as you scale.

Whether you're a founder or a functional lead with a bit of autonomy, these resources will help you move from "AI sounds cool" to "AI is already saving us hours."

You'll find both of these downloads at the link provided in the introduction, or visit the URL below to access them now.

https://www.doublepeakpublishing.com/savvy-guide-ai-beginners-3-smart-bonuses

Pro Tip: Test before you invest. Most tools offer free versions or trials—use them to validate value before you commit.

7.3 YOUR MOST POWERFUL TEAMMATE: HOW TO BUILD A CUSTOM GPT THAT WORKS LIKE YOU DO

If there's one AI tool that small teams and entrepreneurs should priori-tize, it's a custom GPT. Why? Because it's flexible, scalable, and surprisingly easy to build—especially with tools like OpenAI's ChatGPT.

Imagine having a virtual teammate trained on your brand voice, your product details, your tone, and your priorities. A custom GPT can:

- Generate content aligned with your style and structure
- Answer customer questions based on your specific offerings
- Assist in operations by interpreting data or streamlining reports
- Speed up creative workflows like brainstorming or editing

It's also one of the most accessible ways to get the benefits of retrieval-augmented generation (RAG)—a technique you may remember from earlier chapters. RAG is what enables many enter-prise-grade AI systems to pull in real-time, business-specific informa-tion to deliver smarter, more context-aware answers. With a custom GPT, small teams can achieve similar results on a smaller scale by uploading relevant knowledge, documents, and guidance into the model's memory.

And unlike off-the-shelf tools that lock you into pre-defined work-flows, a custom GPT can adapt to *your* processes, *your* team, and *your* goals.

Let's look at what this actually looks like in practice—because the real power of a custom GPT isn't just in theory, it's in the time it saves and the quality it delivers.

WHAT USED TO TAKE DAYS NOW TAKES MINUTES: A REAL-WORLD WIN

Creating case studies usually takes days—interviews, transcription, drafting, editing. But with a custom GPT trained on our brand voice and process, we've streamlined the entire workflow—and even have AI conducting the interview itself. Here's how we use it:

- A human interviewer or a custom GPT conducts structured interviews with the team involved in the project
- We upload the full transcript (whether from an AI interview or a human one) directly into our custom case study GPT for processing
- The GPT drafts the full case study in our preferred format and asks the user for approvals and clarification along the way
- The user iterates on the draft in-chat, refining tone, structure, and flow in real time
- Stakeholders from the project team review the case study for accuracy
- Writers finalize the piece with only light human editing before design handoff

My team cut case study production time by 70% for ourselves and our clients—all while keeping our case studies authentic and on-brand.

So, how can you build a GPT that works like this for your own team? It's easier than you think. Below is a simplified framework to help you get started with a high-impact, low-friction custom GPT.

BUILD YOUR TEAMMATE: A SIMPLE GUIDE TO GETTING STARTED

1. **Define Your Objective** – Start by identifying a single high-impact task. Do you need help drafting emails? Writing job descriptions? Responding to customer FAQs?
2. **Prepare Your Inputs** – Collect example outputs, brand guidelines, tone-of-voice notes, and any content your GPT should emulate or draw from. Think of this as onboarding your AI teammate.
3. **Use ChatGPT's Custom GPT Builder** – OpenAI's no-code interface makes it easy. You'll walk through steps to upload

files, describe behavior, and train your GPT on your content and needs.

4. **Test and Refine** – Run your new GPT through real use cases. Provide feedback by fine-tuning prompts or updating its system instructions. This is where iteration drives value.

5. **Deploy Thoughtfully** – Use your GPT inside ChatGPT or connect it to your workflows using tools like Zapier or low-code platforms.

For a deeper dive into creating your own custom GPTs, don't miss the bonus guide that comes with this book.

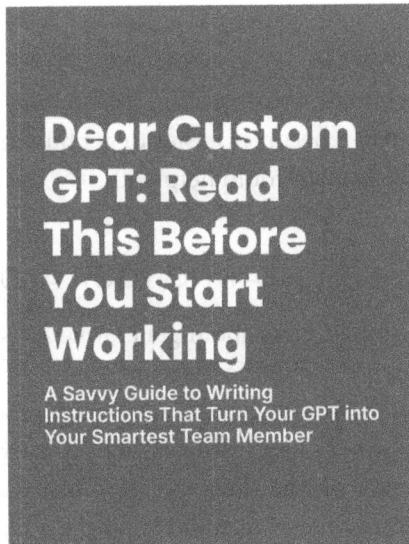

Bonus Resource: Dear Custom GPT: Read This Before You Start Working. A Savvy Guide to Writing Instructions That Turn Your GPT into Your Smartest Team Member

This practical guide helps you go from "uh...what is it doing?" to "wow, it works like it's been on my team for years." Inside, you'll find:

- Sample inputs and training materials
- Prompt templates to get started faster

- System instruction examples that set the tone and boundaries
- Tips for aligning your GPT with your brand and iterating for continuous improvement

Whether you're building a simple assistant or scaling custom GPTs across your team, this bonus will help you write clearer instructions, structure knowledge effectively, and avoid common missteps.

You can download this bonus along with the others using the link in the book's introduction or by visiting it now:

https://www.doublepeakpublishing.com/savvy-guide-ai-beginners-3-smart-bonuses

Pro Tip: Start with one clear use case. Expand from there. Once you see results in one area, it becomes easier to get buy-in—and to imagine what else your AI teammate could help with.

7.4 THINK BIGGER: CREATING YOUR AI DREAM TEAM

One of the most exciting things about generative AI is just how much it can do for small teams and entrepreneurs. Once you get the hang of building custom GPTs, you're not only boosting productivity—you're also saving money by avoiding pricey subscriptions to multiple tools.

The truth is, many off-the-shelf tools are just user-friendly wrappers around the same generative AI technology. While those platforms can be convenient, they often lock you into narrow use cases and fixed workflows. Custom GPTs, on the other hand, let you set the rules. Instead of adapting your processes to fit a tool, you can shape a tool to fit your processes.

The only real limit? Your imagination.

Whether you want to streamline operations, enhance customer experiences, or support strategic decision-making, a custom GPT can help you get there.

Here are some creative ways small teams are already using GPTs:

- **Content Creation Assistant** – Generate blog posts, social media content, and marketing materials in your brand's unique voice.
- **Customer Support AI** – Automate responses to FAQs, assist with troubleshooting, or guide new customers through onboarding.
- **Project Management Helper** – Build a GPT that creates project plans, tracks deadlines, and sends reminders.
- **Data Analysis Expert** – Interpret reports, extract insights from sales data, and generate analytics summaries.
- **Interviewing AI** – Conduct structured interviews to gather content for case studies or internal assessments.
- **Creative Brainstorming Partner** – Generate fresh ideas for campaigns, product features, or new business opportunities.
- **Training and Onboarding Coach** – Help new employees learn about your company culture, tools, and processes in an interactive way.
- **Strategic Thought Partner Committee** – Simulate a panel of virtual experts (marketing, ops, finance, HR) to help stress-test decisions and refine ideas.

So what's next after building one helpful GPT? Building *more*—and getting them to work together. What if you didn't just have one AI assistant—but a whole AI support team?

That's the concept behind creating an *AI Dream Team*. Instead of relying on one general-purpose GPT, you assign different GPTs to different business functions, each tailored to its domain. Marketing. Operations. Customer Service. Strategy. These aren't pie-in-the-sky ideas—they're already working for real teams.

BIG IMPACT, SMALL TEAM: THE 3-GPT BUSINESS BLUEPRINT

Consider a small e-commerce company with just three employees. By integrating three custom GPTs, each focused on a core business function, they boosted efficiency and cut down on repetitive tasks:

- **Marketing GPT** – Generates social posts, email campaigns, and product descriptions—keeping everything aligned with brand voice.
- **Operations GPT** – Analyzes sales data, suggests reorder schedules, and supports inventory planning.
- **Customer Support GPT** – Offers templated responses to FAQs, supports tone-consistent replies to escalated issues, and even drafts onboarding instructions.

Each GPT is trained with business-specific data and documentation—so their outputs are useful, on-brand, and ready to go.

How to Build Your Own AI Dream Team

1. **Identify Your Business Functions** – Start with the major workflows in your business—marketing, customer service, internal ops, analytics, product.
2. **Choose High-Impact Use Cases** – What's repetitive, slow, or hard to delegate? That's where GPTs shine.
3. **Create Specialized GPTs** – Use OpenAI's custom GPT builder to craft assistants that reflect the tone, priorities, and data specific to each area.
4. **Test, Learn, and Expand** – You don't need to build all your GPTs at once. Prove the value of one, then scale.

What to Automate—and What to Keep Human

As you scale your AI team, be thoughtful about boundaries. AI is great at pattern recognition, summarization, and structured creativity. But it's still not great at nuance, context-switching, or making judgment calls.

Automate:

- Repetitive content creation
- Standard reporting
- Structured customer responses
- Data summarization and analysis

Keep human:

- High-stakes communication
- Final creative direction
- Strategy decisions
- Relationship-building and empathy-driven work

Pro Tip: Let AI do the grunt work, so you can focus on growth. Use it to clear the runway—then bring your human creativity and insight in for takeoff.

Next Up: how to build a culture of AI curiosity—even if you don't have a dedicated tech team.

7.5 BUILDING AN AI CULTURE WITHOUT A TECH TEAM

You don't need an enterprise IT department to build momentum with generative AI—you just need the right mindset and a little structure. That's where the *Mini-CoE* comes in.

In the previous chapter, we explored how Centers of Excellence (CoEs) can help guide generative AI efforts in larger organizations, often involving cross-functional teams, compliance oversight, training plans, and formal governance.

But what does that look like when you're not part of a large enterprise—or you're a small team operating independently within one? That's what we're zooming in on here. Because yes, the CoE concept scales down beautifully. With a few key moves, even a team of one or two can borrow the best parts of a CoE and put them to work—without bureaucracy, and without needing to be technical.

WHAT'S A MINI-CoE?

It's a lightweight framework for AI experimentation. One or two people (not necessarily technical) take the lead on exploring tools, running small tests, documenting what works, and sharing learnings with others. Their job isn't to "own AI"—it's to spark curiosity, lower barriers, and make experimentation easy.

Step 1: Designate an AI Champion

This doesn't need to be someone with "innovation" in their title. Your AI champion just needs to be:

- Curious about AI
- Willing to try new things
- Comfortable sharing what they learn

Ideally, they're embedded in day-to-day work—not floating above it. That way, they can spot opportunities for AI to save time, reduce friction, or add value.

Step 2: Keep It Simple and Visible

Start small: one tool, one process, one team. Set a clear goal, like "Cut the time it takes to draft internal reports in half."

Then, document it. Not in a fancy report—just a Google Doc or Notion page with three columns:

- What we tried
- What happened
- What we learned

Invite others to contribute their own experiments and outcomes. This creates a lightweight, living library of what works (and what doesn't).

Step 3: Show the Wins

Skepticism is normal—especially if your team worries about privacy, ethics, or job displacement. The best way to shift that mindset is to show how AI makes their lives easier, not harder.

Look for quick wins that:

- Reduce busywork
- Eliminate frustrating tasks
- Help people focus on more creative or strategic work

These wins build confidence and credibility. They're the fuel that helps your AI culture grow.

Pro Tip: Wins build trust faster than hype. Don't overpromise what AI can do. Just let the results speak for themselves.

Next Up: A practical roadmap to help you get started—your first 30 days with AI.

7.6 YOUR FIRST 30 DAYS WITH AI: A QUICKSTART ROADMAP

So you're ready to try generative AI. You've got ideas, maybe even a curious teammate or two—but now you're wondering where to start.

This section lays out a simple, low-risk plan to get you from zero to traction in 30 days. No need to overhaul your workflows or master every tool. Just start where you are, test what's useful, and build from there.

Week 1: Identify Your First Use Case

- Pick one high-friction task that drains time or creative energy (e.g., writing status updates, responding to customer FAQs, summarizing long docs).
- Talk with your team: Where are the bottlenecks? What's repetitive? What do people wish they had help with?
- Choose a starting point that's low risk but high reward—a task where AI can add immediate value.

Week 2: Pick a Tool and Test It

- Try a few free or low-cost options from the *Smart Stack for Small Teams and Entrepreneurs* list (see downloadable resource).
- Or build a basic custom GPT in ChatGPT with simple instructions and sample outputs.
- Run your selected use case with the tool. Compare the AI output with your current workflow—how does it stack up?
- Start collecting observations: Was it faster? Was it accurate? What surprised you?

WEEK 3: REFINE AND EXPAND

- Tweak your prompts, templates, or instructions to get better results. (We'll go much deeper into the art and science of prompt engineering in the next chapter, so don't worry if you're just getting started.)
- Test the tool in a few related tasks. If you started with social copy, try email drafts. If you started with data analysis, try dashboards.
- Start tracking time saved or quality improvements— anything that builds your case for continued use.

WEEK 4: SHARE THE WINS AND PLAN NEXT STEPS

- Create a short recap (1-pager or Slack post): what you tried, what worked, what you'll do next.
- Share it with your team—or your manager—to show progress and invite collaboration.
- Choose your next experiment. This might be:
  - Training a custom GPT for a second use case
  - Testing a more advanced tool
  - Getting feedback from teammates on where they'd like support

Remember: Progress > perfection. Your goal isn't to become an AI expert in 30 days. It's to learn something useful, spark some ideas, and lay the groundwork for a smarter, more efficient way of working.

Pro Tip: Just start. Curiosity and momentum matter more than knowing everything upfront.

Next Up: How to keep up the momentum—and turn small wins into lasting change.

7.7 FINAL THOUGHTS: THINK SMALL, WIN BIG, TURN EXPERIMENTS INTO TRANSFORMATION

Generative AI isn't just a time-saver. It's creative leverage—especially for small businesses and nimble teams who know how to move fast and think big.

If there's one key message to take away from this chapter, it's this: You don't need a big team to make a big impact. You just need the curiosity to explore, the initiative to start small, and the persistence to build on your wins.

Start with one experiment. Share what you learn. Create one custom GPT. Build a Mini-CoE. Run a 30-day sprint. Then do it again.

That's how transformation starts—not with a sweeping overhaul, but with a single, smart step forward.

The question now is: What will you create?

If you've made it this far, you're not just dabbling—you're building something meaningful. You've explored tools, built your first custom GPT, maybe even started shaping an internal AI culture.

But there's one skill that ties it all together—and determines how effective your results will be moving forward: prompting.

In the next section, we'll dive into the art and science of prompt engineering: what it is, why it matters, and how to master it to get dramatically better outputs from generative AI tools. Whether you're writing a customer response, building a strategy bot, or creating an AI-powered onboarding guide, the right prompt is where precision and potential meet.

And prompting is just the beginning. You'll also explore how to collaborate with AI creatively—so it doesn't just follow instructions, but actually helps you think better, write better, and build ideas you wouldn't have landed on alone.

The tools are powerful. But the real transformation happens when you bring your curiosity, creativity, and craft to the table. That's what we're covering next.

PART FOUR

GETTING REALLY, REALLY GOOD AT IT

This is where it gets fun. You'll learn how to prompt like a boss and team up with AI in ways that make your work better—not more robotic. Spoiler: Your creativity still matters (a lot).

EIGHT

PROMPT LIKE A PRO (BECAUSE AVERAGE PROMPTS GET AVERAGE RESULTS)

magine you're on a business trip in a country where you don't speak the language. You know a few phrases—enough to order a coffee or find the bathroom—but not enough to negotiate a deal or hold a deep conversation. That's what it's like using generative AI without knowing how to prompt it well. You'll get something back, sure. But will it be what you actually *need*? Probably not.

Prompting is how we talk to AI. And more importantly, it's how we *guide* AI. Whether you're asking for a product description, a market analysis, or your next big campaign idea, the quality of your prompt directly shapes the quality of the response. In fact, crafting prompts with purpose is often the difference between an output that's flat and one that's freakishly good.

This chapter is your hands-on guide to becoming fluent in AI's language. You'll learn:

- How generative AI *thinks* (Spoiler: It's not thinking in the way you do.)
- A toolbox of essential and advanced prompting techniques
- How to combine prompting methods for better business results

- Common pitfalls to avoid, and
- Exercises to sharpen your skills as you go.

Prompt engineering isn't just a technical trick. It's a new kind of literacy for the modern workplace. And it might just be your unfair advantage.

8.1 THE PROMPTING MINDSET: THINK LIKE AN AI WHISPERER

Before you start crafting prompts like a pro, you need to shift how you think about talking to AI. Because while it may feel like you're chatting with a super-intelligent assistant, the truth is more mechanical and less magical.

Generative AI doesn't *understand* your words. It doesn't know your business, your goals, or your context. What it *does* know is how to predict the next most likely word based on trillions of examples it saw during training. Think of your prompt like a GPS: It's not about being poetic or verbose; it's about giving clear directions to help the AI find the best path forward.

This means a few mindset shifts are in order:

Be Specific, Not Vague

"Write a report" is like asking for a ride without saying where you want to go. "Write a 500-word report analyzing Q3 sales trends with two recommended actions for Q4" gives the AI a route to follow.

Provide Context

AI doesn't know what's in your head. If your prompt assumes background knowledge it doesn't have, you'll get generic results. Feed it the background it needs, just like you would a new team member.

Embrace Iteration

The first draft won't always be gold. That's not a bug—it's the process. Prompting is a dialogue, not a one-shot command. Try something, assess, revise, and re-prompt. That back-and-forth is where the real progress happens.

Once you adopt this mindset, prompting becomes less about learning a "hack" and more about developing a strategic way of thinking. It's less *talking to a machine*, and more *co-creating with a capable (but literal) partner*.

In the next section, we'll dig into the specific prompting techniques that bring this mindset to life—with plenty of examples and practice you can put to work immediately.

8.2 ESSENTIAL TECHNIQUES: SMARTER PROMPTS START HERE

GET CLEAR, GET RESULTS

Clarity + Specificity = Better Output

If you've ever gotten a response from AI that felt like it belonged in a fortune cookie—vague, surface-level, and basically useless—it probably wasn't the AI's fault. It was the prompt.

Let's fix that.

Example (Weak): "Write a summary."
Example (Better): "Write a 200-word summary of our Q3 customer satisfaction survey, highlighting three key insights and at least two specific recommendations for improving our support team's responsiveness."
Why It Works: You're giving the AI just enough constraints to do great work—like a creative brief in miniature.

Instructional Prompting: Guide the Steps

Think of this like project managing the AI. You're not just asking for a result; you're walking it through how to get there.

Example: "Create a project plan for launching our new employee onboarding app. Step 1: Define success metrics. Step 2: Identify key deliverables. Step 3: Draft a communication plan. Step 4: Assign roles and timelines."

Zero-Shot vs. Few-Shot Prompting

Zero-shot – Ask a question with no examples. While specificity usually gets better results (see above!), there are times when vagueness is useful—especially when you're exploring broadly and want to see a range of directions before narrowing in.

Few-shot – Give a few examples so AI knows the vibe or structure you want. Ideal for brand voice and consistency.

Example (Zero-Shot): "Create social captions for our wellness brand."

Example (Few-Shot): "Create social captions for our wellness brand. Examples: 'Less stress. More clarity. That's the goal.' and 'Breathe in. Log off. Realign.' Now write five more."

———

Try This: Pick a task you do regularly—like writing a status update or drafting a client summary. Rewrite your usual prompt using either specificity, instructional prompting, or few-shot prompting. What changed in the output?

GUIDE THE AI's VOICE AND PERSPECTIVE

Persona Prompting: Assign a Role

Want expert-level responses? Tell AI *who* it is.

Example: "Act as a CFO. Analyze this month's expense report and highlight areas for cost optimization."

When you give the AI a role, it channels the tone, priorities, and vocabulary of that persona. It's like inviting a subject-matter expert into the conversation.

Chain-of-Thought Prompting: Ask for the Thinking, Not Just the Answer

Don't just ask AI to "give you a strategy"—ask it to show its work.

Example: "Before recommending a campaign strategy, list current audience engagement trends and explain why each trend matters."

Why It Works: This leads to more thoughtful and logical results—especially for complex tasks that involve nuance or multiple considerations.

REACT Prompting (Basic Version): Reason + Act

REACT stands for Reasoning and Acting in a sequence.

Example: "Analyze our product reviews, identify the top three issues customers mention, and then suggest specific feature improvements to address them."

This technique is great when you want the AI to analyze *and* do something with that analysis—not just summarize.

Try This: Think of a challenge you're facing—like increasing engagement on your team's newsletter. Now write one prompt where AI takes on a role (e.g., content strategist), and another that includes reasoning steps. What did each approach add?

In the next section, we'll combine these prompting techniques in real business scenarios—so you can see how it all comes together to drive sharper insights and better results.

8.3 PROMPTING IN THE REAL WORLD: SCENARIOS THAT ACTUALLY MATTER

Prompt engineering isn't about memorizing formulas or being a tech wizard. It's about knowing how to combine the right techniques at the right time—especially when you're facing real business challenges.

Let's walk through a real-world scenario that shows how mixing and matching prompting techniques can help you generate not just *any* response—but one that's strategic, detailed, and actually useful.

SCENARIO: YOU'RE LAUNCHING A NEW ECO-FRIENDLY PRODUCT AND NEED A FULL MARKETING STRATEGY.

Step 1: Set the Role (Persona Prompting)

"Act as a Chief Marketing Officer (CMO). Create a go-to-market strategy for our new eco-friendly product."

This helps the AI adopt the mindset of a business leader and prioritize strategic insights over surface-level fluff.

Step 2: Guide the Process (Instructional Prompting)

"As a CMO, break the strategy into these steps: 1) Analyze market trends. 2) Identify key customer segments. 3) Propose messaging that highlights sustainability. 4) Recommend a 6-month rollout plan with KPIs."

The instructions add structure to the AI's thinking—so the strategy doesn't come back as a blob of disconnected ideas.

Step 3: Ask for Its Reasoning (Chain-of-Thought Prompting)

"Before diving into the rollout plan, summarize the current trends in eco-conscious consumer behavior and explain why they support this product launch."

Now the AI is not just giving you answers—it's giving you rationale. That's what turns outputs into insights.

Step 4: Iterate for Depth (Iterative Prompting)

Run the prompt. Review what it gives you. Then refine:

"Expand the social media section. Include three platform-specific tactics and an influencer partnership idea that aligns with our brand values."

Prompt, tweak, repeat. This is how you elevate a good AI draft into a great one.

———

Try This: Think of a real challenge you're working on right now—something like preparing for a product launch, writing a proposal, or rethinking a customer journey. Try combining two or more prompting techniques from this chapter. Start broad, get structured, ask for reasoning, then iterate. Watch how the quality and usefulness of the AI's response evolves.

Next, we'll move into the deep end with advanced prompting techniques for bigger, messier, more strategic challenges. (You're ready.)

8.4 GOING PRO: ADVANCED PROMPTING TECHNIQUES

So, you've got the basics down. Your prompts are clear. You've played with personas. You've even gotten AI to break down its reasoning. Now it's time to go pro.

This section is for the deep-thinkers, the strategists, the people solving gnarly business problems where "give me three tips" doesn't quite cut it. The techniques here are your power tools.

Let's break them down—and then see how they can work together in a real-world business scenario.

META PROMPTING: PROMPT THE PROMPT

This is a two-step dance. First, you generate ideas. Then you prompt the AI *again* to reflect, refine, or narrow its focus based on what it just gave you.

Example:
Prompt 1: "Give me five creative ideas for launching a new software product."
Prompt 2: "From that list, pick the two ideas that are most budget-friendly and explain how we could execute them in under 30 days."

Why It Works: You're not accepting the first answer—you're turning the AI into your strategist and your editor.

SELF-CONSISTENCY PROMPTING: GENERATE + COMPARE

Instead of asking for one answer, ask for multiple—and evaluate them against clear criteria.

Example: "Propose three different sales strategies for our Q4 push. For each one, include expected ROI, risk level, and required resources."

Why It Works: You get options, not assumptions. And you can cherry-pick or blend the best parts.

CONTEXTUAL PRIMING: LOAD THE DECK

Feed the AI background info *before* you ask your question. It's like giving your intern a dossier before their first big assignment.

Example: "Here's what we know: 1) EV demand is rising, especially in urban markets. 2) Government subsidies are increasing. 3) Our product has a longer battery life and lower cost. Based on this context, develop a go-to-market strategy."

Why It Works: AI can only use what it knows. And in this case, what it knows is whatever you just told it.

ADVANCED REACT PROMPTING: THINK FIRST, THEN DO

We touched on REACT earlier. This version adds layers.

Example: "Analyze the challenges in our supply chain over the past year. Then recommend three changes to improve efficiency *and* reduce cost. For each one, include potential risks and mitigation tactics."

Why It Works: It turns AI into a full-on analyst—not just a glorified text generator.

PUTTING IT ALL TOGETHER: A BUSINESS SCENARIO

Scenario: Your Company Is Entering the Electric Vehicle (EV) Market

Let's apply all four techniques:

Step 1 – Contextual Priming
"Our EV is designed for city use, with a 20% longer battery range than competitors. The target audience is urban professionals. Government incentives are making EV adoption easier, but we're entering a crowded space."

Step 2 – Meta Prompting
"Generate five market entry strategies for this EV."

Follow-up: "From these, choose the most cost-effective one and break it down into a 90-day launch roadmap."

Step 3 – Self-Consistency Prompting
"Create three launch campaign concepts. For each one, estimate the marketing spend, channels to prioritize, and expected reach."

Step 4 – Advanced REACT Prompting
"Review the top campaign idea. List three reasons it could fail. Then suggest ways to reduce those risks while maintaining impact."

This is where prompt engineering goes from helpful to high-impact. You're not just asking AI for outputs. You're running a strategic planning session—with a bot that doesn't get tired or need coffee.

———

Try This: Take a current challenge (maybe it's launching a product, opening a new market, or fixing a broken process). Prime the AI with context. Generate ideas. Narrow with meta prompts. Compare with self-consistency. Then analyze risks with REACT. Watch how much further this takes you than a single-shot prompt.

Next, we'll look at how to avoid common pitfalls that can trip up even seasoned prompters.

8.5 AVOID THE USUAL PITFALLS (AND HOW TO FIX THEM)

Even the savviest prompt pros hit snags now and then. The good news? Most AI misfires aren't the AI's fault—they're the result of vague, bloated, or just plain confusing prompts.

Let's fix that.

Here are the top five prompting mistakes I see most often—along with mini makeovers to help you course-correct fast.

MISTAKE #1: THE FRANKEN-PROMPT

Prompt
"Write a sales report, summarize customer feedback, and draft an email to the team."

Why It Misses
You've packed multiple unrelated asks into one prompt. This isn't just a long prompt—it's a disjointed one. The tasks aren't clearly connected, which makes it harder for AI to prioritize or create a cohesive response.

Makeover
Break it up. One task per prompt. "Generate a Q3 sales report summary focusing on regional performance." Then: "Summarize customer feedback on our Q3 product launch." Then: "Write a team email summarizing both."

MISTAKE #2: THE MYSTERY PROMPT

Prompt
"Write an article about how AI can improve productivity."

Why It Misses
This gives AI a general direction but not enough detail. What kind of productivity? For whom? In what context? The result will likely be vague and high-level—something you could've Googled.

Makeover
Get more focused: "Write a 600-word article for HR leaders on how generative AI can help reduce time spent on employee

policy documentation. Use a friendly, expert tone and include one example of a company already doing this."

MISTAKE #3: THE MIND-READER

Prompt
"Create a plan for our new project."

Why It Misses
AI doesn't know what your new project is unless you tell it. No context = a generic plan that won't hit the mark.

Makeover
Feed the details. "Create a project plan for our internal chatbot rollout to assist employees with IT support questions. Include key milestones and training timelines."

MISTAKE #4: THE MEGA-PROMPT

Prompt
"Write a 10-slide deck summarizing financials, product performance, customer feedback, competitor updates, and our 2025 strategy."

Why It Misses
This one's more about density than disconnection. All the elements are related, but cramming them into a single prompt without hierarchy or structure overwhelms the AI—and you get a sprawling, unfocused result.

Makeover
Chunk it out. "Start with a 3-slide summary of Q3 financials. Include key wins, red flags, and one visual chart suggestion." Then build each section with separate, focused prompts.

MISTAKE #5: THE ONE-AND-DONE

Prompt
"Write a proposal for our new consulting service."

Why It Misses
Even if the first draft is decent, it's not optimized. You're missing the opportunity to iterate and sharpen.

Makeover
Use a second prompt: "Improve clarity in the intro. Add one customer quote as a proof point. Make the close more persuasive."

———

Try This: Go find a prompt you've used recently—something real. Check it against this list. Can you tighten it up? Split it? Add missing context? Run the new version and see what changes.

Fixing even one of these mistakes can turn a frustrating prompt into one that delivers gold.

Coming up next: exercises to help you practice everything you've learned so far.

8.6 THE PROMPT WARM-UP: REPEATABLE EXERCISES TO KEEP YOUR SKILLS SHARP

You've made it through a ton of techniques—and you've probably tried a bunch already. This section isn't just practice for practice's sake. It's a hands-on warm-up for using prompting in real, everyday business scenarios. Think of it like stretching before a big pitch, strategy session, or content sprint.

Here's how it works: Each level includes a scenario you can make your own, a recommended mix of techniques to try, and an example of one way to approach it well. You can compare what you did to the example—and sharpen your instincts along the way.

BEGINNER: CLARITY, SPECIFICITY, AND STRUCTURE

Scenario to Try
You need to send a weekly update to your manager about the team's progress. It's often hard to know what to include, and it sometimes feels too generic.

Techniques to Use

- Instructional prompting
- Clarity and specificity

Your Turn
Start by providing the AI with a few bullet points or a brief list of what happened that week—accomplishments, challenges, or plans. The more grounded input you give it, the more useful the result will be.

To help the AI do its job well, you can also upload or reference:

- Last week's update (to maintain consistency)
- A project tracker or task list
- Meeting notes or a Slack summary

Example
Prompt:
"Write a 150-word weekly update email to my manager summarizing team progress. I've included notes below. Please include 1) key accomplishments, 2) blockers, and 3) upcoming priorities. Use a professional but conversational tone."
Notes:

- The new onboarding feature rollout was completed ahead of schedule on Wednesday; no major bugs reported.
- We're waiting on final budget approval for two new hires (roles already scoped).
- Customer success flagged a rise in support tickets related to mobile UI—could be worth investigating.

- Goal for next week: Launch an internal survey to gather team feedback on the new feature and identify process bottlenecks.

INTERMEDIATE: LAYERED ROLES AND PLANNING

Scenario to Try
You're planning an internal initiative—like updating your onboarding process—and need a roadmap to get buy-in and make it happen.

Techniques to Use

- Persona prompting
- Instructional prompting
- Chain-of-thought prompting

Your Turn
Before prompting, provide relevant internal context to help the AI tailor its response. You might include:

- Your current onboarding process steps or checklist
- Feedback from recent hires
- Employee retention stats for the first 90 days
- Common complaints or confusion points in onboarding
- Goals for improving new-hire experience or efficiency

Example
Prompt:
"Act as an HR project manager. Before recommending a plan, identify the top three problems in our current onboarding process and explain why each one is worth fixing. Then outline a 5-step plan to improve the experience, including a brief rationale for each step. Use the notes below as background."
Notes:

- We currently use a basic Google Doc checklist; onboarding tasks are often missed or completed late.
- Recent hire feedback mentioned lack of clarity on team roles and scattered resources.
- 30% of new hires report confusion about tools and systems in the first month.
- We want to make onboarding more engaging and structured to support a growing team and reduce time to productivity.

ADVANCED: STRATEGIC THINKING WITH MULTIPLE LAYERS

Scenario to Try
You're evaluating whether to expand into a new market segment (e.g., mid-sized healthcare providers) and want help thinking through risks, messaging, and go-to-market planning.

Techniques to Use

- Contextual priming
- Self-consistency prompting
- REACT prompting
- Meta prompting

Your Turn
To help the AI give you strategic, relevant guidance, consider uploading or referencing:

- A summary of your current customer base and usage data
- Notes from previous expansion discussions or executive briefings
- A market research snapshot or industry trends doc
- Recent sales or marketing performance reports
- Known constraints (e.g., team size, marketing budget, tech stack)

Then, guide the AI through generating and comparing strategies, identifying risks, and recommending next steps.

Example

Prompt 1 – Contextual Priming + Self-Consistency Prompting:
"We're a SaaS company that helps healthcare organizations streamline patient scheduling. Our core customers are large hospital systems, but we're considering expanding into mid-sized outpatient clinics. We've noticed that sales cycles are longer with smaller organizations, and our onboarding experience is optimized for larger IT teams. Our current GTM strategy focuses on white-glove service and enterprise sales outreach. We're debating whether it's worth shifting strategy to reach this new segment.

Generate three different go-to-market strategies for launching our scheduling platform to mid-sized healthcare providers. For each, include target messaging themes, recommended channels, estimated cost range, and expected ROI."

→ This prompt primes the AI with detailed context and asks it to generate multiple structured options so the user can compare.

Prompt 2 – REACT Prompting:
"Now, for the most promising strategy from above, identify the top three risks or challenges we might encounter. Then propose one mitigation tactic for each."

→ This gets the AI to analyze *and* respond—reasoning first, acting second.

Prompt 3 – Meta Prompting:
"Now take the selected GTM strategy and simplify it for a team with limited marketing resources and no dedicated sales reps. Adjust the plan while preserving impact."

→ Here, the AI reflects on and adapts its own output, showing strategic refinement.

USE AND REUSE

Each of these scenarios is meant to be flexible. Swap in your own real project. Try different mixes of prompting strategies. Make your own versions. And revisit often.

The more you prompt with intention, the faster you'll go from *getting something usable* to *getting something amazing.*

Use this section as your go-to warm-up. Or your troubleshooting station. Or your AI thinking partner's training gym. However you use it—just keep using it.

8.7 WRAP-UP: OWN THE PROMPT, LEVEL UP YOUR CAREER

By now, you've seen that prompting isn't just a one-off skill—it's a mindset shift, a creative strategy, and a serious career differentiator.

You've learned how to:

- Think like an AI whisperer, not a taskmaster.
- Structure prompts with clarity, context, and intention.
- Combine prompting techniques—like personas, instructional prompting, and REACT—for sharper results.
- Iterate, experiment, and refine like a pro.

And most importantly, you've practiced how to move from vague requests to specific, actionable, high-quality outputs.

Prompt engineering isn't just about coaxing better words from a machine. It's about collaborating with AI in a way that multiplies your thinking, speeds up your work, and elevates your output—no matter your role.

So before you move on, pause for a moment:

What's one thing you'll do differently the next time you prompt?

Maybe you'll slow down and clarify your goal first. Maybe you'll set the stage with context. Maybe you'll think of the prompt as a conversation, not a command.

Whatever it is, own it. That's how this becomes second nature.

In the next chapter, we'll take prompting even further—into the world of creative collaboration. We'll explore how to co-create with AI to generate ideas, solve problems, and develop original work you'll actually be proud to sign your name to.

Let's go.

NINE

KEEP IT CREATIVE: HOW TO WORK WITH AI WITHOUT LOSING THE SOUL OF YOUR WORK

If you've ever had a knee-jerk reaction to someone using AI for creative work—maybe something along the lines of, "That's just plagiarism with extra steps," or "Well, anyone can do that," or "That's not real creativity"—you're not alone.

The backlash is real, and it's passionate. There's a prevailing fear that machines are elbowing their way into the creative sandbox and will soon take over. And on the flip side, there's an equally loud chorus claiming that generative AI doesn't replace creativity; it amplifies it. But what does that actually mean? And how do we, as humans, stay creative *with* AI without losing the soul of our work?

That question matters more than ever—because creativity isn't just one more thing AI can do. It's what defines this entire era of AI.

Unlike previous generations of AI, which focused on analysis, optimization, and prediction, generative AI does something fundamentally different: It creates. It produces text, images, music, code, even new ideas. And that leap—from prediction to creation—is why it's changed the game. It's also why it's created such intense debate, especially among artists, designers, writers, and other creative professionals.

That's why this chapter exists. Not because creative work is the only thing generative AI can do—but because it's the thing that makes it *generative*. It deserves more than hot takes or hand-wringing. It deserves real consideration, real tools, and real conversation.

So that's what we're doing here.

We're not here to rehash the legal debates or ethics of AI-generated content—we covered that already. What we're doing here is rolling up our sleeves and exploring how to *work* with AI creatively. Not theoretically, but practically. Not in a way that dilutes your authenticity, but one that strengthens it. Not to cut corners, but to open new doors.

Because creativity has never been a solitary act. It's always been shaped by collaboration, technology, iteration, and the tools at hand. AI is just the newest tool—and perhaps the most powerful one yet. The key is not whether we use it, but *how* we use it.

And sometimes, the best lessons about working with AI don't come from tech at all. They come from classrooms, conversations, and even a group of skeptical students staring down a blank page. More on that soon.

9.1 CREATIVITY ISN'T DYING—IT'S EVOLVING

Every era of innovation has met with skepticism from creatives. When photography emerged in the 1800s, some painters declared it the death of fine art. When synthesizers and digital audio hit music production, purists mourned the end of "real" musicianship. And when animation studios began using computers to assist with everything from backgrounds to full character motion, there were fears that it would sap the magic out of the medium. Spoiler: It didn't.

In fact, it did the opposite.

The introduction of technology has never killed creativity. It has shifted where it lives.

Take animation, for example. Before computer-assisted tools, animators drew every frame by hand—an awe-inspiring craft that demanded years of practice, precision, and imagination. But it was also incredibly labor-intensive. When digital tools entered the scene, they didn't eliminate all artistry, but they did shift the nature of it. Artists devoted more energy to character development, visual storytelling, emotional nuance, and dynamic world-building, while technology handled the repetitive or time-consuming parts. The result? More creative freedom, faster iteration, and an explosion of new visual possibilities.

The same pattern is unfolding with generative AI.

AI doesn't make creativity obsolete, but it does shift where the human effort goes. Instead of pouring all our energy into starting from scratch, we focus more on strategy, refinement, storytelling, and emotional resonance. AI becomes a new kind of collaborator: one that never gets tired, always has ideas, and is happy to iterate endlessly.

Collaboration, after all, has always been at the heart of creation. From co-writers to creative teams to editors and art directors, the most impactful work often comes from building off of one another. Generative AI is just the latest creative partner. And like any partner, it's not about what it can do on its own—it's about what you can do together.

Up next, I'll share one of the most unexpectedly useful lessons I've ever learned about collaboration—and it didn't come from a lab or a studio. It came from a group of students in a college writing class, learning how to co-create something meaningful, one paragraph at a time.

9.2 BEFORE GENERATIVE AI WAS EVEN A THING, MY STUDENTS SHOWED ME WHAT IT'S LIKE TO COLLABORATE WITH IT

Years ago, while teaching a writing class at UC Berkeley, I designed an experiment. I asked students to write in small groups—not to critique each other's drafts, but to create them collaboratively, from scratch. The idea was intentional but a little unconventional: We'd break down a larger writing project into sections, study great examples, then work together to write each section as a team. I wasn't sure exactly how it would go. I hoped it might spark deeper engagement or bring out new kinds of creative thinking. But what unfolded surprised me in ways I couldn't have fully anticipated.

You might be picturing chaos. And at first, it kind of was.

Some students groaned when they heard the plan. Others looked politely confused. This wasn't how they had been taught to write.

Writing was supposed to be solitary, deeply personal—you go off alone, pour your soul onto the page, and only then do you invite others in. This new approach felt, to some, like it would water down their voice or result in bland compromise.

Even a fellow professor observing the session was skeptical. She circled the room, watching groups scribble, debate, erase, start over. Later, she admitted, "I didn't think this was going to work. But by the end, I could see how deeply they were engaging. It was surprisingly effective."

It worked because we didn't just throw students into the deep end. Each group first dissected examples of strong writing. They explored what made the work compelling, what gave it voice, and how structure supported meaning. Then they wrote their own takes on small sections—first individually, then as a group. They compared approaches, combined the best of each, and iterated until the section felt tight, purposeful, and original.

What emerged wasn't bland or watered down. It was layered. It was richer than any single draft because it reflected multiple perspectives, refined through conversation and revision.

And here's the part that connects to AI: This experience taught me that originality doesn't come from isolation. It comes from interaction.

When people worry that AI will make our work generic, what they're often picturing is a world where humans take the first suggestion AI spits out and call it done. But that's not collaboration. That's outsourcing. The real power of working with AI comes when you treat it like a room full of creators who never run out of ideas, don't mind doing dozens of iterations, and never get precious about their drafts.

Like those student groups, you can dissect examples together, try different versions, compare approaches, and blend the best parts. And yes, argue a little. That friction is often where the best ideas come from.

AI doesn't have to erase your voice. But it can challenge it. It can sharpen it. It can push you into creative corners you wouldn't have wandered into alone.

And that's the point. Collaboration isn't the opposite of originality. In many cases, it's the birthplace of it.

9.3 CREATIVE CHEMISTRY: WHAT HAPPENS WHEN HUMANS AND AI TEAM UP

To make this real, I want to show you how this collaboration actually looks in practice. One of these stories made headlines. The others are more personal—but no less powerful. Together, they show how humans can stay in charge, stay creative, and still say yes to the tools of the future.

AI MEETS HAUTE COUTURE: HOW LULU LI USED AI IN FASHION DESIGN

In 2023, luxury brand Moncler collaborated with Chinese artist and designer Lulu Li to create a ready-to-wear fashion collection that merged AI-generated concepts with human craftsmanship. Li, who had been experimenting with AI tools to simulate fashion collections, used generative AI to draft initial designs, lookbooks, and even conceptual runway presentations.

For this project, she generated creative prototypes aligned with Moncler's aesthetic, then worked closely with their technical team to translate those designs into wearable garments. One standout piece—a cream puffer gown showcased at Moncler's "City of Genius" event in Shanghai—was born from this collaboration. The process required navigating AI-generated hallucinations and adapting conceptual outputs into technically viable fashion pieces.

The result was a capsule collection that blended speed and innovation with intentional, human-led refinement. AI didn't design the collection on its own. But it sparked fresh possibilities that were then shaped by skilled hands into something truly couture.

ELISA'S VISUAL LIBRARY: WHEN CONSTRAINTS INSPIRE INNOVATION

Our creative director, Elisa, has been quietly mastering the art of using AI in ways that preserve authenticity in her design work. That skill proved invaluable when she led a project for a global client facing a major design challenge: They needed a custom visual library to showcase their manufacturing capabilities, but strict confidentiality agreements meant they couldn't use actual photos of the high-profile parts and products they create. Traditionally, this would mean scouring stock image libraries and investing significant time in Photoshop wizardry to cobble together something brand-aligned.

Instead, Elisa turned to AI.

Using MidJourney, she and her team generated a range of original visuals based on detailed prompts about the products and the brand's aesthetic and needs. They didn't stop there. The team treated the AI outputs like concept art—reviewing, selecting, and refining the best ones using traditional design tools. They enhanced details, adjusted lighting, and added the subtle touches that made each image feel intentional and on-brand.

The result? A unique visual library that not only respected confidentiality constraints but actually pushed the brand's visual identity forward. The AI didn't just solve a problem. It elevated the creative opportunity.

My Co-Writing Experience: Where Drafting Meets Dialogue

The last time I wrote a full-length book, generative AI didn't exist—and writing was a lonely, solitary process. Sure, once I had a draft, I'd ask trusted colleagues to read and comment. And yes, I had editors to help shape the final structure. But the day-to-day work of writing? That was mine alone.

In my professional life, though, it's a different story. I work with full creative teams—designers, writers, UX professionals, engineers (who I firmly believe *belong* on creative teams)—and our work is stronger because we build it together. The best ideas are shaped, challenged, and elevated in that shared space. Collaboration doesn't just make the work more creative; it makes it more alive.

So when I set out to write this book—a personal project without the usual team behind me—I expected to go it alone again. But this time, I had generative AI.

From the earliest brainstorming sessions to full drafts, a custom GPT I trained on my notes, research, and voice became my behind-the-scenes writing partner. It helped me generate ideas, pressure-test assumptions, and rework sections from different angles. Sometimes its suggestions were laughably off, which helped me clarify what I *didn't* want to say. Other times, it offered phrasing or perspectives I hadn't thought of—little sparks that lit up whole new sections.

One of the most unexpectedly creative moments came when I asked it to critique my outline through the eyes of different reader personas. That single exercise reshaped how I structured the book—and deepened my connection to you, the reader.

I was still the writer. The final voice, content, decisions, and structure were all mine. But the process felt more collaborative than solitary. More like a creative jam session than a solo grind.

Generative AI didn't water down my creativity, but it did help me sharpen it. It didn't do the work for me, but it did push me to do better work. And in that way, it made the process *more* human, not less.

———

These stories illustrate something powerful: When used thoughtfully, AI can be a catalyst for better, more expansive creative work. Whether you're designing visuals, developing a brand narrative, or writing a book, collaboration with AI can deepen your creative process. The secret lies in how you engage with it: not as a shortcut, but as a partner in exploration.

9.4. KEEP IT REAL: HOW TO COLLABORATE WITH AI WITHOUT LOSING THE SPARK

If you've made it this far, you've probably picked up on a theme: Authentic creativity doesn't have to disappear when AI enters the picture—it can actually thrive. But only if we engage with AI thoughtfully, intentionally, and with a clear sense of purpose. This isn't just about how to use AI tools. It's about how to stay rooted in your creative values while adapting to new capabilities.

In fact, the principles that make AI collaboration effective are the same ones that drive great human collaboration. Whether you're co-writing a screenplay, building a brand identity with a design team, or brainstorming campaign concepts in a conference room, the creative truths still hold. AI just brings a tireless partner to the table—one that's always game for another round of ideas and never takes feedback personally.

Here are five enduring principles for working with AI that apply across disciplines. Think of them not just as tech guidance, but as creative wisdom for any kind of team-based work.

1. TRY. TWEAK. REPEAT.

Great ideas rarely arrive fully formed. In any creative team, the first draft is never the last—and working with AI is no different. Like a brainstorming partner who never runs out of suggestions, AI helps you move quickly through multiple versions, unlocking new directions you might not have found alone. The value lies not in the first idea, but in what you build from it.

2. KEEP YOUR HANDS ON THE WHEEL

Every strong creative team needs someone to guide the vision. With AI, that's you. Just like working with a junior designer, a co-writer, or a strategist, the best collaborations come from clear direction and thoughtful refinement. Let AI contribute ideas, but remember: You're the one steering the ship.

3. LET IT STIR THE POT

In the same way a colleague might toss out a wild idea that unlocks your best thinking, AI can prompt unexpected angles or challenge your assumptions. It's not about turning over the wheel. It's about letting AI stir the pot so your own creative instincts can respond in sharper, more interesting ways.

4. GO FAST, BUT DON'T FAKE IT

Creative teams often rely on each other to speed things up without cutting corners. AI is no different. Yes, it can help you go faster. But meaningful work still demands a human heartbeat. Use AI to move quickly through mechanical steps—just like a teammate handling the first draft or research summary—but make sure your voice and vision still shine through.

5. GET CURIOUS, NOT PRECIOUS

The best collaborations encourage experimentation. And AI's ability to generate limitless options makes it a dream partner for that. Treat it like the teammate who always says, "What if we tried it this way?"—then explore freely, knowing that even a wild idea might spark the breakthrough you were waiting for.

———

These principles aren't just about generative AI—they're about how creativity works in real life. When you treat AI as a creative partner instead of a threat or shortcut, you open the door to faster break-throughs, richer exploration, and more meaningful results. The future of creative work *can* still be led by humans—if we choose to lead it. AI gives us a collaborator who never runs out of energy, but it's up to us to shape how that collaboration unfolds.

9.5 PRACTICE MAKES CREATIVE: HANDS-ON AI COLLABORATION EXERCISES

Reading about creative collaboration with AI is one thing. Experiencing it is something else entirely.

The first time I really understood the power of AI in a creative workflow wasn't when I was writing a chapter or designing a prompt —it was during a moment of total frustration. I was stuck trying to title a new framework for a client. Nothing sounded right. Everything felt either too generic or too clever for its own good. Out of options, I fed a loose description into my AI assistant. Not for the perfect answer, but for *something* to react to. Within minutes, I had twenty imperfect but promising ideas—and two that helped me land on the final title. It wasn't magic. It was momentum.

That's the point of these exercises. Not to show off what AI can do, but to get you moving, thinking, and creating in new directions. Use them as creative warm-ups or real workflow tools—whatever works for you.

Exercise 1: Brainstorming With AI

Tool Recommendation
ChatGPT, Jasper, Copy.ai

Try This
Give the AI a prompt related to your current project.

Example: "Generate 10 fresh campaign ideas for a wellness brand launching a new sleep product."

Review the outputs. Highlight anything that sparks a reaction. Use those highlights to build something better. Combine, refine, reframe.

Mini-Challenge
Spend 10 minutes asking the AI for variations. Then spend another 10 combining the best bits into a pitch or concept.

Advanced Move
Ask the AI to play devil's advocate: "What are the weaknesses in this concept?" or "Challenge my assumptions here." It forces you to sharpen your ideas.

Exercise 2: Design Exploration With AI

Tool Recommendation
MidJourney, Adobe Firefly, Canva's AI features

Try This
Enter a specific, vivid prompt.

Example: "Create a product mockup inspired by brutalist architecture and 1970s color palettes."

Review the results. Pull what resonates. Refine it using your favorite design tools—Photoshop, Illustrator, Figma, etc.

Mini-Challenge
Generate five different versions. Pick one and push it through three iterations.

Advanced Move
Experiment with unexpected inputs: "Visualize the idea of joyful resistance," or "Design a homepage inspired by jazz improvisation." Surprise yourself.

EXERCISE 3: ITERATIVE WRITING WITH AI

Tool Recommendation
ChatGPT, Claude, or a custom GPT

Try This
Write a short paragraph or description. Ask AI for suggestions to expand, tighten, or rewrite.

Compare outputs. Keep what works, toss what doesn't. Merge ideas into a refined draft.

Mini-Challenge
Use the same prompt 3 ways: once for clarity, once for tone, once for structure. Combine the best elements.

Advanced Move
Ask the AI to rewrite your paragraph from different points of

view. Or try, "What would this sound like in a TED talk?" to test tone and impact.

Exercise 4: Problem-Solving With AI

Tool Recommendation
ChatGPT, Gemini, or Copilot

Try This
Present a challenge.

Example: "How can I build a sense of community into my remote onboarding process?"

Ask for five solutions. Then ask for pros and cons. Use what resonates to map out next steps.

Mini-Challenge
Pick one AI suggestion. Draft a plan to test it.

Advanced Move
Prompt the AI to pressure-test your plan: "What are the risks?" or "What might I be overlooking?" Let it challenge you.

Reflect and Refine

After each exercise, take a moment to note what felt easy, surprising, or frustrating. That's part of the process, too. The goal here isn't perfection. It's movement. It's discovery.

The more you work with AI like a creative partner—curious, experimental, open to iteration—the more you'll unlock its potential. Not by letting it think for you, but by inviting it to think *with* you.

9.6 CREATIVITY AMPLIFIED—IF YOU CHOOSE IT

Here's the truth: AI won't take your creativity unless you let it. It's offering to collaborate. What you do with that offer is entirely up to you.

You can ignore it, fear it, or resist it. Or you can meet it with curiosity and intentionality. You can choose to make it a tool that strengthens your thinking, broadens your reach, and invites new dimensions into your creative process.

Because AI doesn't have a creative agenda. You do.

Every example in this chapter—from fashion and visual design to writing and strategic problem-solving—has shown how AI can amplify human creativity when we use it well. Not passively. Not blindly. But with the same mindset we bring to any great creative collaboration: openness, rigor, exploration, and taste.

The exciting part? This is still unfolding. There is no rulebook. No one right way to work. And no ceiling on what's possible. Which means you have the opportunity to define your own path. To shape a practice that reflects your values and voice—with AI as a creative partner, not a threat.

You don't have to be a technologist to shape the future of creativity. You just have to show up with a willingness to explore, to experiment, and to stay grounded in what matters most to you.

So take what you've learned here, and start.

Try a new tool. Tweak a prompt. Ask a weird question. Run a draft past an AI assistant. Challenge it. Let it challenge you back.

You have more power than you think. The future of creativity doesn't belong to AI—it's shaped by what we choose to do with it. You have the opportunity to lead it, shape it, and decide what comes next.

TEN

THIS ISN'T THE END—IT'S YOUR STARTING LINE

We've covered a lot of ground—from demystifying generative AI to getting our hands dirty with prompts, workflows, and real-world use cases. But if we've done this right, this isn't the end of the journey. It's a starting line.

The shift ahead isn't just technical. It's a mindset shift. One where AI isn't something we react to, but something we shape. It doesn't make the decisions unless we hand them over. We do.

When used well, AI isn't a gimmick or a shortcut. It's the endlessly curious, always-available teammate that helps you push past creative blocks, accelerate your process, and expand what you thought was possible. It won't replace your voice—unless you let it. It helps you find it, faster. And make it louder.

But AI only does what we ask it to. That means we have an incredible opportunity—and responsibility—to guide it with intention. To apply it ethically. And to use it in ways that amplify not just efficiency, but humanity.

What We Know Now

We know that AI literacy is no longer optional. If you understand what AI is good at—and what it isn't—you're not just keeping up. You're leading.

We know that ethics can't be an afterthought. Creativity without integrity won't take us anywhere worth going.

And we know that human insight is still the X factor. AI can generate a thousand ideas. But only you know which one matters.

What Comes Next

For Professionals
Start integrating AI into your workflows. Not because you have to. But because it makes you faster, sharper, and more strategic.

For Leaders
Champion thoughtful experimentation. Build a culture that rewards curiosity, protects accountability, and supports learning.

For Everyone
Talk about it. Share what you're learning. Ask better questions. The more we normalize responsible use, the stronger our collective future becomes.

Imagine What's Possible

Imagine generative AI helping a nonprofit translate life-saving health information into dozens of languages overnight. Scientists generating new scenarios that could uncover unexpected pathways to restoring our planet. A teacher in a rural community co-creating personalized learning paths to unlock opportunities for every student.

These aren't distant dreams. They're glimpses of what's already beginning to happen when we choose to point this technology toward real human needs.

And the most exciting part? The most powerful applications haven't even been dreamed up yet. That's your invitation.

ONE LAST THOUGHT

From my experience building enterprise AI systems, guiding teams, and helping people like you navigate this space, I can tell you this: Real change doesn't come from mastering the tools. It comes from choosing how we use them.

So experiment. Iterate. Take what you've learned in these pages and do something unexpected with it. And when you hit a wall, ask AI for a starting point. Just don't let it finish the story for you.

The future isn't arriving fully formed. We're shaping it. And every thoughtful choice you make with AI brings us one step closer to a world where technology doesn't just make us more efficient—it helps us be more creative, more curious, and more deeply human.

Let's build that future. Together.

AI CAN'T LEAVE REVIEWS—
BUT YOU CAN

If you found yourself nodding, highlighting, or thinking *"Whoa, this is actually useful,"* I'd be *so* grateful if you'd leave a ★★★★★ review wherever you bought this book.

It helps more than you might think.

Platforms notice those stars and say, *"Ah, yes. People are into this. Let's show it to more humans."* (Okay, maybe not in those exact words. But close.)

Your review doesn't need to be long. Just honest.

Thanks for reading. For sharing. For building something smarter with AI. And thanks especially for supporting this book.

JAMIE DEANGELIS
Author + Human
Still prefers real stars to algorithmic ones. But both are appreciated.

REMINDER: **Don't forget to grab your three smart bonuses! They're yours, and they're waiting for you:**
https://www.doublepeakpublishing.com/savvy-guide-ai-beginners-3-smart-bonuses

ACKNOWLEDGMENTS

Writing a book about something as fast-moving, unpredictable, and occasionally unhinged as generative AI is like trying to capture lightning in a mason jar. (Except the lightning keeps updating itself, and the jar occasionally hallucinates facts.)

I couldn't have done it alone.

To my husband: You said, *"Hey, OpenAI just released this thing called custom GPTs. We should make some!"* And just like that, you kicked off my obsession. Thank you for that. Also: sorry. Because from that moment on, you had to endure countless AI ramblings over coffee, dinner, and probably in your sleep. You created a monster. A curious, caffeinated, very chatty monster.

To Dan Williams, my CEO and the rare kind of leader who doesn't just *talk* about innovation—he makes space for it. Thank you for trusting me enough to explore this generative frontier, fumble around, experiment wildly, and ultimately lead our Generative AI Center of Excellence. None of this happens without that gift of space, support, and belief.

To the engineers who helped me understand how all this actually works: Yuji Minegishi, Kyle Holloway, and everyone else who patiently walked me through things like token limits and transformer architecture without ever once asking, *"Wait ... aren't you the brand and content person?"* You made me feel like I had a seat at the table—and a reason to be there.

To Elisa Anguiano—creative explorer, brilliant designer of this book's cover, and one of the most fun co-conspirators in testing the outer limits of what AI can do when paired with human imagination.

Thank you for making this journey beautiful, brainy, and just the right amount of weird.

To those who read early drafts and offered feedback, encouragement, or emoji reactions that I 100% took as validation: especially Blake Park, who I'm pretty sure read every single word (even the boring parts, bless you).

To my dear friend Sally Soricelli, who reminded me again and again that this thing I was writing mattered—even when I wasn't sure myself. Everyone should have a Sally in their corner.

And finally, to you—yes, *you*—reading this now. Thank you for being curious. For showing up. For giving this little book and its slightly-obsessed author your time and attention. May it spark something for you, the way this journey sparked something for me.

ABOUT THE AUTHOR

Jamie DeAngelis is a former UC Berkeley instructor turned brand strategist, content expert, and generative AI leader helping shape how businesses actually use this technology in the real world. After trading academia for the fast-moving world of business, she built a career helping companies—from global manufacturers to digital agencies—find their voice, tell better stories, and untangle complex ideas without making people's eyes glaze over.

Today, she leads strategic positioning and AI innovation at a boutique agency, where she helps clients navigate the beautifully messy intersection of technology and humanity. She believes content strategists are the unsung heroes of the AI era—and while this book isn't just for them, it's certainly written with their superpowers in mind (crafted, of course, with structure, style, and a dash of editorial nerdiness).

When she's not wrangling prompts or brand frameworks, Jamie's cheering on her kids at the ballfield, playing a slightly chaotic round of golf with her husband, or lavishing attention on her golden retriever. She lives in sunny San Diego, where beach days are plentiful and her husband moonlights as a volunteer snake wrangler—yes, really—heroically saving suburban homeowners from panic, and rattlesnakes from a worse fate. Jamie mostly contributes moral support … and a steady stream of deeply concerned commentary. Retirement goals include fewer fangs, more baguettes, and a quiet French village with excellent wine and absolutely no Slack messages.

BIBLIOGRAPHY

CHAPTER 1: WAIT, WHAT IS GENERATIVE AI, EXACTLY?

1 "Exploring the Shift from Traditional to Generative AI," The Curve, MIT, accessed April 14, 2025. https://curve.mit.edu/exploring-shift-traditional-generative-ai.

CHAPTER 2: MYTHS, MISUNDERSTANDINGS, AND THAT ONE WILD AI MEETING

1 Blake Brittain, "Meta Hit with New Author Copyright Lawsuit over AI Training," Reuters, October 2, 2024. https://www.reuters.com/legal/litigation/meta-hit-with-new-author-copyright-lawsuit-over-ai-training-2024-10-02/.

CHAPTER 3: WHAT COULD GO WRONG? (LET'S TALK ABOUT IT.)

1 Natasha Lomas, "Samsung Bans Use of Generative AI Tools like ChatGPT after April Internal Data Leak," TechCrunch, May 2, 2023. https://techcrunch.com/2023/05/02/samsung-bans-use-of-generative-ai-tools-like-chatgpt-after-april-internal-data-leak/.
2 Feven Merid and Nicholas Diakopoulos, "AI Search Has a Citation Problem," Columbia Journalism Review, September 26, 2023. https://www.cjr.org/tow_center/we-compared-eight-ai-search-engines-theyre-all-bad-at-citing-news.php.
3 Dan Milmo, "CEO of World's Biggest Ad Firm Targeted by Deepfake Scam," The Guardian, May 10, 2024. https://www.theguardian.com/technology/article/2024/may/10/ceo-wpp-deepfake-scam.
4 Alexander S. Gillis, "Is AI-Generated Content Copyrighted?" TechTarget, accessed April 14, 2025. https://www.techtarget.com/searchcontentmanagement/answer/Is-AI-generated-content-copyrighted.
5 "What Is a Prompt Injection Attack?" Wiz Academy, accessed April 14, 2025. https://www.wiz.io/academy/prompt-injection-attack.

CHAPTER 4: ETHICAL AI ISN'T A TECH PROBLEM. IT'S A PEOPLE PROBLEM.

1 Katie Paul, "UN Advisory Body Makes Seven Recommendations for Governing AI," Reuters, September 19, 2024. https://www.reuters.com/technology/artificial-intelligence/un-advisory-body-makes-seven-recommendations-governing-ai-2024-09-19/.
2 Michael Brewer and Nancy Olson, "AI Tug-of-War: Trump Pulls Back Biden's AI Plans," The Employer Report, January 25, 2025. https://www.theemployerreport.com/2025/01/ai-tug-of-war-trump-pulls-back-bidens-ai-plans/.
3 "AI Risk Management Framework," National Institute of Standards and Technology (NIST), accessed April 14, 2025. https://www.nist.gov/itl/ai-risk-management-framework.

4 "The Global Partnership on Artificial Intelligence," GPAI, accessed April 14, 2025. https://gpai.ai/.

5 "High-Level Advisory Body on Artificial Intelligence," United Nations Office for Digital and Emerging Technologies, accessed April 14, 2025. https://www.un.org/digital-emerging-technologies/ai-advisory-body.

6 Andrew Boryga, "How AI Will Impact the Future of Teaching—a Conversation With Sal Khan," *Edutopia*, November 27, 2024. https://www.edutopia.org/article/how-ai-will-impact-the-future-of-teaching-a-conversation-with-sal-khan.

CHAPTER 5: FROM HYPE TO HELP: WHAT GENERATIVE AI IS REALLY GOOD AT

1 "International Program," *Khan Academy Annual Report 2023–24*, accessed April 14, 2025. https://annualreport.khanacademy.org/international-program.

2 "From Start to Phase 1 in 30 Months: AI-Discovered and AI-Designed Anti-Fibrotic Drug Enters Phase I Clinical Trial," Insilico Medicine, accessed April 14, 2025. https://insilico.com/phase1.

3 Anton Shilov, "Synopsys Intros AI-Powered Suite to Accelerate Chip Design and Cut Costs," *AnandTech*, September 20, 2023. https://www.anandtech.com/show/18798/synopsysai-aipowered-eda-suite-accelerates-chip-design-and-cuts-costs-.

4 Andrew R. Chow, "How One Company Is Using 3D Printing and AI to Make Sports Cars More Efficiently," *Time*, November 16, 2023. https://time.com/7023380/czinger-3d-print-ai-sports-car/.

5 "Coca-Cola Creations Imagines Year 3000 with New Futuristic Flavor and AI-Powered Experience," Coca-Cola Company, September 12, 2023. https://www.coca-colacompany.com/media-center/coca-cola-creations-imagines-year-3000-futuristic-flavor-ai-powered-experience.

6 Sarah Johnston, "How U.S. Cities Are Using AI to Solve Common Problems," *Harvard Business Review*, December 2024. https://hbr.org/2024/12/how-u-s-cities-are-using-ai-to-solve-common-problems.

7 Tao Wang, Huanan Li, Bin Zhou, Yuming Fang, and Liangzhi Li, "A Review of Generative Artificial Intelligence Applications in Renewable Energy Systems," *Applied Energy* 354 (2024): 122313. https://www.sciencedirect.com/science/article/pii/S0306261925000261.

8 Leslie Dickstein, "How AI Is Being Used to Respond to Natural Disasters in Cities," *Time*, March 28, 2024. https://time.com/7171445/ai-natural-disaster-cities/.

9 "Mass General Brigham Research Identifies Pitfalls and Opportunities for Generative Artificial Intelligence in Patient Messaging Systems," Mass General Brigham, January 25, 2024. https://www.massgeneralbrigham.org/en/about/newsroom/press-releases/pitfalls-and-opportunities-for-generative-ai-in-patient-messaging-systems.

10 "Synthetic Data for Real Insights," JPMorgan Chase, accessed April 14, 2025. https://www.jpmorgan.com/technology/technology-blog/synthetic-data-for-real-insights.

11 "13 Ways to Use Generative AI in R&D and IP," Evalueserve, accessed April 14, 2025. https://www.evalueserve.com/blog/13-ways-to-use-generative-ai-in-rd-and-ip/.

12 Zofia Zwieglinska, "Designing Fashion in the AI Era," *Glossy*, April 1, 2024. https://www.glossy.co/fashion/designing-fashion-in-the-ai-era/.

CHAPTER 6: CUSTOM AI FOR ENTERPRISE—HOW TO BUILD IT RIGHT, NOT JUST BUY IT FAST

1 Jamie DeAngelis, "In the Age of AI, Data Is Your New Content Strategy — Are You Ready?" *BRINK Interactive*, February 27, 2024. https://brinkinteractive.com/how-we-think/in-the-age-of-ai-data-is-your-new-content-strategy-are-you-ready/.

2 Yuji Minegishi, "The True Differentiator in AI Projects: Intelligent Engineering," *BRINK Interactive*, March 26, 2024. https://brinkinteractive.com/how-we-think/the-true-differentiator-in-ai-projects-intelligent-engineering/.

3 "Inside the BRINK Generative AI Center of Excellence — Where Strategy, Technology, and Creativity Merge to Drive Smarter AI Solutions," *BRINK Interactive*, April 9, 2024. https://brinkinteractive.com/how-we-think/inside-the-brink-generative-ai-center-of-excellence-where-strategy-technology-and-creativity-merge-to-drive-smarter-ai-solutions/.

CHAPTER 8: PROMPT LIKE A PRO (BECAUSE AVERAGE PROMPTS GET AVERAGE RESULTS)

1 Lilian Weng, "Prompt Engineering," *Lil'Log*, March 15, 2023. https://lilian-weng.github.io/posts/2023-03-15-prompt-engineering/.

2 "Prompt Engineering Guide," *LearnPrompting.org*, accessed April 14, 2025. https://learnprompting.org/docs/introduction.

3 "Prompt Engineering Guide," *The Prompting Guide*, accessed April 14, 2025. https://www.promptingguide.ai/.

CHAPTER 9: KEEP IT CREATIVE: HOW TO WORK WITH AI WITHOUT LOSING THE SOUL OF YOUR WORK

1 Karen Chernick, "'From Today Painting Is Dead': Photography's Revolutionary Effect," *Art & Object*, February 5, 2021. https://www.artandobject.com/news/today-painting-dead-photographys-revolutionary-effect.

2 "Photography as Art, Painting as Impression," *Dawn's Early Light* exhibition, Cornell University Library, accessed April 14, 2025. https://rmc.library.cornell.edu/Dawns-EarlyLight/exhibition/art/index.html.

3 Bryn Stole, "The Fear That Synthesizers Would Ruin Music," *JSTOR Daily*, August 7, 2023. https://daily.jstor.org/the-fear-that-synthesizers-would-ruin-music/.

4 Jonathan Watts, "A God Among Animators," *The Guardian*, September 14, 2005. https://www.theguardian.com/film/2005/sep/14/japan.awardsandprizes.

5 *Kati Chitrakorn, "Style vs Craft: Turning AI Designs into IRL Clothes," Vogue Business, February 27, 2024. https://www.voguebusiness.com/story/fashion/taste-vs-craft-turning-ai-designs-into-irl-clothes.*